AF761356

ECONOMIC ISSUES, PROBLEMS AND PERSPECTIVES

INTERNATIONAL PERSPECTIVES ON FINANCIAL MARKET SUPERVISION

ECONOMIC ISSUES, PROBLEMS AND PERSPECTIVES

Additional books in this series can be found on Nova's website under the Series tab.

Additional E-books in this series can be found on Nova's website under the E-books tab.

ECONOMIC ISSUES, PROBLEMS AND PERSPECTIVES

INTERNATIONAL PERSPECTIVES ON FINANCIAL MARKET SUPERVISION

JAMES P. CORRIGAN
EDITOR

Nova Science Publishers, Inc.
New York

Copyright © 2011 by Nova Science Publishers, Inc.

All rights reserved. No part of this book may be reproduced, stored in a retrieval system or transmitted in any form or by any means: electronic, electrostatic, magnetic, tape, mechanical photocopying, recording or otherwise without the written permission of the Publisher.

For permission to use material from this book please contact us:
Telephone 631-231-7269; Fax 631-231-8175
Web Site: http://www.novapublishers.com

NOTICE TO THE READER

The Publisher has taken reasonable care in the preparation of this book, but makes no expressed or implied warranty of any kind and assumes no responsibility for any errors or omissions. No liability is assumed for incidental or consequential damages in connection with or arising out of information contained in this book. The Publisher shall not be liable for any special, consequential, or exemplary damages resulting, in whole or in part, from the readers' use of, or reliance upon, this material. Any parts of this book based on government reports are so indicated and copyright is claimed for those parts to the extent applicable to compilations of such works.

Independent verification should be sought for any data, advice or recommendations contained in this book. In addition, no responsibility is assumed by the publisher for any injury and/or damage to persons or property arising from any methods, products, instructions, ideas or otherwise contained in this publication.

This publication is designed to provide accurate and authoritative information with regard to the subject matter covered herein. It is sold with the clear understanding that the Publisher is not engaged in rendering legal or any other professional services. If legal or any other expert assistance is required, the services of a competent person should be sought. FROM A DECLARATION OF PARTICIPANTS JOINTLY ADOPTED BY A COMMITTEE OF THE AMERICAN BAR ASSOCIATION AND A COMMITTEE OF PUBLISHERS.

Additional color graphics may be available in the e-book version of this book.

LIBRARY OF CONGRESS CATALOGING-IN-PUBLICATION DATA

International perspectives on financial market supervision / editor, James P. Corrigan.
p. cm.
Includes index.
ISBN 978-1-61728-006-1 (softcover)
1. Securities industry. 2. Banks and banking--Government ownership--Case studies 3. Financial institutions--State supervision--Case studies. 4. Markets--Law and legislation. I. Corrigan, James P.
HG4521.I378 2010
332.64--dc22

2010014115

Published by Nova Science Publishers, Inc. ✝ New York

CONTENTS

PREFACE

The global financial crisis has sparked a debate over the cause and impact of the crisis. Academics and policymakers are searching for changes in the financial system that can correct any perceived weaknesses in the structure of regulation, the content of regulations, and the coverage of financial instruments and activities. Since the onset of the crisis, numerous proposals have been advanced to reform or amend the current financial system to help restore economic growth. This new book addresses the international perspectives on a number of proposals that are being advanced for financial oversight and regulation in the global financial markets and promoting integration and consistency across the various financial structures.

Chapter 1 - Federal financial regulation in the United States has evolved through a series of piecemeal responses to developments and crises in financial markets. This chapter provides an overview of current U.S. financial regulation: which agencies are responsible for which institutions and markets, and what kinds of authority they have.

Chapter 2 - The global financial crisis has sparked a debate over the cause and impact of the crisis. Academics and policymakers are searching for changes in the financial system that can correct any perceived weaknesses in the structure of regulation, the content of regulations, and the coverage of financial instruments and activities. Since the onset of the crisis, numerous proposals have been advanced to reform or amend the current financial system to help restore economic growth. In the United States, the Obama Administration has proposed a plan to overhaul supervision of the U.S. financial services sector. The proposal would give new authority to the Federal Reserve, create a new Financial Services Oversight Council, create a Consumer Financial Protection Agency, and create a new National Bank Supervisor to replace the Office of the Comptroller of the Currency and the

Office of Thrift Supervision. In contrast, Senator Collins introduced S. 664, the Financial System Stabilization and Reform Act of 2009, with a companion measure, H.R. 1754, that was introduced by Representative Castle in the House of Representatives. The measures would create a Financial Stability Council and grant the Federal Reserve the authority to examine the soundness and safety of the financial system posed by bank holding companies. Other measures include: S. 1682 (Senator Cantwell), the Derivatives Market Manipulation Prevention Act of 2009; S. 1803 (Senator Merkley), the Federal Reserve Accountability Act of 2009; S. 2756 (Senator Warner) the Financial Services Systemic Risk Oversight Council Act of 2009; H.R. 3795 (Representative Frank), the Over-the-Counter Derivatives Markets Acts of 2009; H.R. 3968 (Representative Ellison), to amend the Bank Holding Company Act; and H.R. 3996 (Frank), to improve financial stability. The crisis has underscored the fact that national and international financial markets have become highly integrated, and problems in one market can trigger contagion that can spread both among countries and into economic sectors to affect businesses, employment, and household well being.

Similarly, governments in Europe are considering what, if any, changes they should make to their national financial systems. Along with the United States and other countries, European countries also are considering changes to the international systems of financial supervision and regulation in order to ensure prosperity through the smooth operation of domestic and international financial systems. This process may include reconsidering the roles and responsibility of the central banks in the post-financial crisis era. Various organizations and groups are advancing a large number of recommendations and prescriptions. Some goals for any such adjustments may include providing an institutional structure for oversight and regulation that is robust, comprehensive, flexible, and politically feasible while providing appropriate incentive structures to preclude excessive risk- taking. Of course, there are no guarantees that amending the current system or employing a different regulatory and supervisory structure will preclude a repeat of the most recent financial crisis given that financial markets and institutions are continually growing, innovating, and responding to government- and market-imposed constraints.

This chapter addresses the European perspectives on a number of proposals that are being advanced for financial oversight and regulation in Europe. The European experience may be instructive because financial markets in Europe are well developed, European firms often are competitors of U.S. firms, and European governments have faced severe problems of integration and consistency across the various financial structures that exist in Europe.

Chapter 3 - The international financial crisis has spurred policymakers in the United States and elsewhere to consider changing the way they currently supervise financial institutions and financial markets to reduce the prospects of experiencing another global financial crisis. Canada's financial system, in particular is garnering attention, because it seems to be more resistant to the failures and bailouts that have marked banks in the United States and Europe. In particular, some observers are assessing the merits of the way Canada supervises and regulates its banks, as one possible model for the United States. There likely are aspects of Canada's financial supervisory framework that may offer an approach to supervising financial markets that may be useful for the United States to consider. However, the smaller scope of Canada's financial system and its economy likely lessen the transferability of systems or procedures used in Canada to the vastly more complex U.S. financial system. This chapter presents an overview of Canada's financial system and its supervisory framework and draws some distinctions between that system and the current U.S. framework.

Chapter 4 - The 111th Congress has taken a broad approach to capturing the lessons on financial crises as part of the effort to evaluate possibilities for revamping the U.S. financial regulatory system. Latin America stands out as one region that has survived multiple financial crises, and in the aftermath of such devastation, many countries undertook comprehensive regulatory reform. Although a smaller developing economy, Chile provides one important example. Following two financial crises, one the result of extreme over regulation, the other of catastrophic under regulation, Chile redesigned its regulatory system in 1986. Since then, it has had one of the most stable financial systems in Latin America and has overcome regional and global financial crises when other countries in the hemisphere did not. In so doing, new-found soundness of the banking system has not compromised bank profitability, reflecting modernization and efficiency gains that paralleled development of effective prudential regulation and oversight.

In: International Perspectives on Financial... ISBN: 978-1-61728-006-1
Editor: James P. Corrigan © 2011 Nova Science Publishers, Inc.

Chapter 1

WHO REGULATES WHOM? AN OVERVIEW OF U.S. FINANCIAL SUPERVISION*

Mark Jickling and Edward V. Murphy

SUMMARY

Federal financial regulation in the United States has evolved through a series of piecemeal responses to developments and crises in financial markets. This chapter provides an overview of current U.S. financial regulation: which agencies are responsible for which institutions and markets, and what kinds of authority they have.

There are two traditional components to U.S. banking regulation: deposit insurance and adequate capital. Commercial banks accept a quid pro quo that was adopted in response to widespread bank failures during the 1930s. Through deposit insurance, the federal government provides a safety net for some banking operations and in return the banks that are exposed to depositor runs accept federal regulation of their operations, including the amount of risk they may incur. Since the 1860s, federal banking regulation has sought to prevent excessive risk taking by banks that might seek to make extra profit by reducing their capital reserves—at the time called "wildcat" banks. There are

* This is an edited, reformatted and augmented version of a CRS Report for Congress publication dated December 2009.

five federal bank regulators, each supervising different (and often overlapping) sets of depository institutions.

Federal securities regulation is based on the principle of disclosure, rather than direct regulation. Firms that sell securities to the public must register with the Securities and Exchange Commission (SEC), but the agency has no authority to prevent excessive risk taking. SEC registration in no way implies that an investment is safe, only that the risks have been fully disclosed. The SEC also registers several classes of securities market participants and firms, but relies more on industry self-regulation than do the banking agencies. Derivatives trading is supervised by the Commodity Futures Trading Commission (CFTC), which oversees trading on the futures exchanges, which have self-regulatory responsibilities as well. There is also a large over-the-counter (off-exchange) derivatives market that is largely unregulated.

The Federal Housing Finance Agency (FHFA) oversees a group of government-sponsored enterprises (GSEs)—public/private hybrid firms that seek both to earn profits and to further the policy objectives set out in their statutory charters. Two GSEs, Fannie Mae and Freddie Mac, were placed in conservatorship by the FHFA in September 2008 after losses in mortgage asset portfolios made them effectively insolvent. A number of financial markets are unregulated, including some of the largest. No federal agency has jurisdiction over trading in foreign exchange or U.S. Treasury securities; nonbank lenders fall outside the regulatory umbrella; and hedge funds, private equity firms, and venture capital investors are largely unregulated (although their transactions in securities and derivatives markets may be).

The United States has never attempted a wholesale reformation of the entire regulatory system comparable to the 1986 "Big Bang" in the UK, which reorganized regulatory agencies across industry lines and sought to implement a consistent philosophy of regulation. In the wake of the current financial turmoil, however, such a reevaluation is possible, and a number of broad restructuring proposals have already come forward.

In the 111th Congress, H.R. 4173 presents comprehensive reform of the banking agencies, derivatives regulation, investor protection, systemic risk, and other concerns. In the Senate, a committee print by Senator Dodd containing comprehensive reform was issued on November 16, 2009.

INTRODUCTION

Historically, major changes in financial regulation in the United States have often come in response to crisis. Thus, one could have predicted that the turmoil beginning in 2007 would lead to calls for reform. A number of studies and reports have already proposed broad changes to the division of supervisory authority among the various federal agencies and in the tools and authorities available to individual regulators. For example, H.R. 4173, the "Wall Street Reform and Consumer Protection Act of 2009," would overhaul the financial regulatory structure. A committee print issued by Senator Dodd on November 16, 2009, the "Restoring American Financial Stability Act," would also provide comprehensive reform of the regulatory system. These legislative efforts follow on the heals of two major proposals by the Treasury Departments of President Bush and President Obama.[1] This report provides a basis for evaluating and comparing such proposals by setting out the basic structure of federal financial regulation as it stood at the beginning of the 111th Congress.

Few would argue that regulatory failure was solely to blame for the current crisis, but it is widely considered to have played a part. In February 2009, Treasury Secretary Timothy Geithner summed up two key problem areas:

> Our financial system operated with large gaps in meaningful oversight, and without sufficient constraints to limit risk. Even institutions that were overseen by our complicated, overlapping system of multiple regulators put themselves in a position of extreme vulnerability. These failures helped lay the foundation for the worst economic crisis in generations.[2]

In this analysis, regulation failed to maintain financial stability at the systemic level because there were gaps in regulatory jurisdiction and because even overlapping jurisdictions—where institutions were subject to more than one regulator—could not ensure the soundness of regulated financial firms. In addition, limits on risk-taking were insufficient. Regulators have a number of risk-reduction tools at their disposal, but the chief one is capital regulation—standards that require firms to maintain capital cushions to protect themselves against unexpected losses.

To create a context for what follows, this report begins with basic analysis of systemic risk and capital regulation. The first section briefly discusses regulatory jurisdiction and systemic risk, and includes a chart listing the major regulators and the types of institutions they supervise. The chart also indicates certain emergency authorities available to the regulators, including those that relate to systemic financial disturbances. The second section focuses on capital requirements and how standards are set by bank, securities, and futures regulators.

The next section provides a brief overview of each of the federal financial regulatory agencies. Because the current crisis is likely to provoke a serious reconsideration of the levels of capital that financial firms should be required to maintain as a cushion against insolvency, the capital standards that each agency applies to various classes of financial firms are also set out.

Finally, the chapter discusses of several major areas of financial markets that are not subject to any federal regulation.

FINANCIAL CRISES, REGULATORY JURISDICTION, AND SYSTEMIC RISK

The United States has experienced several financial panics and economic disruptions in its history. Reactions to financial disruptions have resulted in a complex regulatory framework, in which some agencies have overlapping jurisdictions, and where there may be some regulatory gaps. With each new crisis, including the current one, there are calls to address perceived gaps and weaknesses in the regulatory system. Financial disruptions can originate from at least three sources:

- *failures within the financial system itself*, such as a breakdown in the ability of banks and other financial intermediaries to process their obligations to one another in a timely and efficient manner;
- *demands on the financial system from other sectors of the economy*, such as unexpected pressure on banks to honor their obligations to depositors and investors more quickly than they can accumulate liquid assets; and
- *weakness in real economic sectors*, such as an unexpected drop in the capacity of firms and consumers to repay bank loans.

These three types of problems are illustrated in the Figure 1 and discussed below.

Processes within the Financial Sector

Financial disruptions can manifest themselves within the financial sector itself (represented in the Figure 1 by the numeral 1). For example, banks may have trouble processing checks and other third-party claims, or loans to other banks. Because the willingness and ability of market participants to extend loans and make trades often depends on trust that others will honor their obligations to them in a timely manner, disruptions in interbank lending markets, clearinghouses, and trading exchanges can disrupt financial flows to the wider economy.[3] The Panic of 1857 may represent an instance in which interbank markets failed and contributed to a wider recession—subsequent reforms sought to redress problems within the financial sector itself. Prior to the Civil War, the debts of state-chartered banks circulated as currency. A clearinghouse system was required to process these state bank notes, which often traded at a discount vis-a-vis each other, similar to the way that international currencies today have exchange rates. The value of a state bank note often depended on the perceived safety and soundness of the banks that issued the note. Private inter-bank clearinghouse systems, such as New England's Suffolk Bank, coordinated the processing of bank claims. The Panic of 1857 was a financial crisis in which the value of state bank notes became uncertain and the wider economy suffered a recession. The Suffolk Bank failed in 1858. Partially in response to this crisis, the United States established a single national currency, coordinated through a system of federally chartered banks. The safety and soundness of these banks is regulated by the Office of the Comptroller of the Currency (OCC), established in 1863, as part of banking reforms designed to ease funding of the Civil War.

Honoring Claims of Depositors and Investors

Financial disruptions can result from problems between banks and their sources of funding, whether investors or depositors (indicated by the numeral 2 in the Figure 1). Banks and other financial intermediaries often have a timing mismatch: the value of their assets may only be recoverable over a long period of time, but their liabilities may be subject to immediate repayment. Banks plan for this duration mismatch using a variety of risk-management techniques, but at the end of the day, there are limits to their ability to accommodate changes in investor/depositor behavior. If investors or depositors demand repayment too quickly, a bank may be forced to sell its less liquid assets at a steep discount to meet immediate obligations. The resulting losses, or the fear of such losses, can damage the financial system and cut off credit to the wider economy.

The Panic of 1907 may represent an instance in which banks were unprepared for changes in the behavior of investors and depositors. In 1907, the seasonal increase in demand for currency coincided with disruptions in the New York money market caused by a commodities speculator. F.A. Heinze had used funds from the Mercantile National Bank, which was subject to OCC supervision, in a failed attempt to corner the copper market. Fearing bank insolvency, depositors began a series of runs on institutions believed to be associated with Heinze, including the New York Knickerbocker Bank. During the ensuing liquidity crisis, the swamped OCC staff's response time for currency deliveries slowed down even as demand for money increased. National banks turned to a variety of substitutes for national currency, including the financial resources of investor J.P. Morgan. Partially as a response to this crisis, the United States established a system of federally regulated bank reserves. The Federal Reserve was created in 1914.

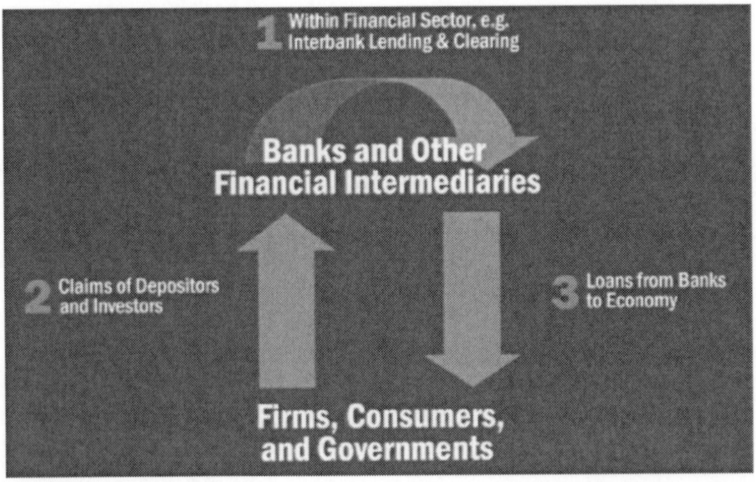

Source: CRS.

Figure 1. Where Financial Disruptions Arise

Table 1. Systemic Crises and the Creation of Financial Regulators

Systemic Event	Perceived Problem	Solution	New Regulator	Year Created
Panic of 1857	Failure of Private Clearinghouses that Processed State Bank Notes (circulated as currency)	Create Single National Currency Through System of Federally Chartered and Regulated Banks	Office of the Comptroller of the Currency (OCC)	1863
Panic of 1907	Series of Runs on Banks and Financial Trusts with Inadequate Reserves	Create Lender of Last Resort with Power to Regulate a National System of Bank Reserves	Federal Reserve	1913
Great Depression	Series of Runs on Banks by Small Depositors who Feared Full Value of Deposits Would Not be Honored	Create Limited Deposit Insurance to Maintain Depositor Confidence and Prevent Bank Runs	Federal Deposit Insurance Corporation (FDIC)	1933
	Sharp Decline in Stock Prices along with Widespread Belief that Some Investors had an Informa-tion Advantage Reduced Confidence in Securities Markets	Restore Confidence in Securities Markets by Standardizing Disclosures and Requiring Regular Reporting	Securities and Exchange Commission (SEC)	1934

Source: CRS.

The Great Depression may represent another episode in which banks were unprepared for changes in depositor behavior. Rising unemployment both increased the need for households to withdraw their savings deposits and reduced the flow of funds into banks through loan repayment. Fear that banks would not be able to honor their commitments to depositors caused a series of bank runs in 1931 and 1933, which forced banks to sell assets at steep discounts. To reduce the likelihood of future bank runs, Congress established a federal insurance program for bank deposits: the Federal Deposit Insurance Corporation (FDIC) was created in 1933.

Performance of Loans from Banks to the Economy

Financial disruptions can also result from worse-than-expected performance of loans from banks to households, businesses, and governments, indicated by the numeral 3 in the figure above. Banks and other financial intermediaries do not expect all loans to be repaid on time and in full; rather, there is always some allowance for loan losses. When loan losses rise above expectations, however, banks become less capitalized. To avoid an undercapitalized system, the OCC and other regulators with safety and soundness authority require subject institutions to prepare for some loan losses. In addition, they examine subject institutions' loan portfolios to assess the overall prudence of lending behavior and attempt to prevent overly risky lending.

During the 2001-2005 housing boom, large volumes of mortgage lending were conducted through non-bank institutions, which were not subject to the prudential lending standards of the bank regulators. Many large banks bought mortgage-backed securities based on such loans—or assumed the equivalent risk exposure through off-balance sheet financing arrangements or derivatives contracts—and have since suffered unexpected losses and become undercapitalized. Some believe that the current crisis is evidence of a regulatory gap, and have called for the establishment of a new systemic risk regulator with authority to oversee all financial institutions and firms that could trigger a systemic disruption.

Thus, new proposals to create a regulator exclusively concerned with systemic risk repeat the pattern that has characterized the development of U.S. financial regulation. The term "systemic risk" does not have a single, agreed-upon definition. Some define systemic risk as the risk an institution faces that it cannot diversify against. In other circumstances, systemic risk is defined as the risk that the linkages between institutions may affect the financial system as a whole, through a dynamic sometimes referred to as contagion. These definitions are compatible in some cases; for example, the linkages between financial institutions could prevent any single lender from effectively protecting itself from problems that emerge in the system as a whole.

The two definitions do not always apply to the same circumstances. Particular institutions in some sectors might face risks that are not diversifiable and that arise from sources other than the financial system. Similarly, linkages between institutions can create aggregate risks that individual institutions could hedge against if they chose to do so, but there is no assurance that the institutions would. In fact, another way to think about systemic risk is that it arises because all market participants have incentives to limit their own risk-taking to prevent loss of the own capital, but no participant will willingly limit its risk-taking—the source of its profitability—to reduce the possibility of a systemic disruption.

Table 2. Federal Financial Regulators and Who They Supervise

Regulatory Agency	Institutions Regulated	Emergency/Systemic Risk Powers	Other Notable Authority
Federal Reserve	Bank holding companies,[a] Financial holding companies, state banks that are members of the Federal Reserve System, U.S. branches of foreign banks, foreign branches of U.S. banks	Lender of last resort to member banks (through discount window lending). In "unusual and exigent circumstances" the Fed may lend to "any individual, partnership, or corporation ... "	The Fed issues consumer protection regulations under various federal laws, including the Truth-in- Lending Act
Office of the Comptroller of the Currency (OCC)	National banks, U.S. federal branches of foreign banks		
Federal Deposit Insurance Corporation (FDIC)	Federally-insured depository institu-tions, including state banks that are not members of the Federal Reserve System	After making a determination of systemic risk, the FDIC may invoke broad authority to use the deposit insurance funds to provide an array of assistance to depository institutions	
Office of Thrift Supervision (OTS)	Federally chartered and insured thrift institutions, savings and loan holding companies		
National Credit Union Adminis-tration (NCUA)	Federally-chartered or insured credit unions	Serves as a liquidity lender to credit unions experiencing liquidity shortfalls through the Central Liquidity Facility	Operates a deposit insurance fund for credit unions, the National Credit Union Share Insurance Fund (NCUSIF)

Table 2. (continued)

Regulatory Agency	Institutions Regulated	Emergency/Systemic Risk Powers	Other Notable Authority
Securities and Exchange Commission (SEC)	Securities exchanges, brokers, and dealers; mutual funds; investment advisers. Registers corporate securities sold to the public	May unilaterally close markets or suspend trading strategies for limited periods	Authorized to set financial accounting standards which all publicly traded firms must use
Commodity Futures Trading Commission (CFTC)	Futures exchanges, brokers, pool operators, advisers	May suspend trading, order liquidation of positions, or raise margins in emergencies.	
Federal Housing Finance Agency (FHFA)	Fannie Mae, Freddie Mac, and the Federal Home Loan Banks	Acting as conservator (since Sept. 2008) for Fannie and Freddie	

Source: CRS.

Notes: For more detail on banking regulation, see the chart "Banking Institutions and Their Regulators," http://www.newyorkfed.org/publications.

a. See Appendix A.

Asset bubbles represent one form of systemic risk. In good times, loans are less likely to default; therefore, it might make sense for any individual bank to increase its leverage and reduce its capital reserves. However, overly easy lending and reduced capital reserves in good times can lead to a bubble in the price of assets financed with loans, such as farms or houses (even tulip bulbs). When the bubble eventually deflates, simultaneous deterioration of banks' balance sheets can result.

Over the years, the financial regulatory system has been modified to address various sources of financial instability and evolving concepts of systemic risk. Not all federal financial regulators have authority to address systemic risk, and no single regulator has jurisdiction over all the financial institutions and markets that may become sources of systemic risk.

Table 2 below sets out the current federal financial regulatory structure: the agencies and the financial institutions they regulate. Supplemental material—charts that illustrate the differences between banks, bank holding companies, and financial holding companies—appears in Appendix A.

CAPITAL REQUIREMENTS

As a general accounting concept, capital means the equity of a business—the amount by which its assets exceed its liabilities.[4] The more capital a firm has, the greater its capacity to absorb losses and remain solvent. Financial regulators require the institutions they supervise to maintain specified minimum levels of capital—defined in various ways—in order to reduce the number of failing firms and to minimize losses to investors, customers, and taxpayers when failures do occur. Capital requirements represent a cost to businesses because they restrict the amount of funds that may be loaned or invested in the markets. Thus, there is a perpetual tension: firms structure their portfolios to reduce the amount of capital they must hold, while regulators continually modify capital standards to prevent excessive risk-taking.

In U.S. banking regulation, capital standards are based on the Basel Accords, an international framework developed under the auspices of the Bank for International Settlements.[5] The guiding principle of the Basel standards is that capital requirements should be risk-based. The riskier an asset, the more capital a bank should hold against possible losses. The Basel Accords provide two broad methodologies for calculating risk-based capital: (1) a standardized approach to credit risk determinations, based on external risk assessments (such as bond ratings), and (2) an alternative approach that relies on banks' internal risk models and rating systems. Adoption of the latter method—set out in the 2004 Basel II framework—in the United States has been slow, and thus far is limited to a few large banks.[6]

Table 3 shows how the standardized approach works in assessing the amount of capital to be held against credit risk in various types of financial instruments. The Basel Accords call for a basic capital requirement of 8% of the value of an asset; the risk-weighting then determines what percentage of that 8% baseline will apply to a given asset. For example, if the risk-weighting is 0%, no capital must be held (i.e., 8% X 0% = 0). A risk weighting of 100% means that the full 8% requirement applies. Assets weighted above 100% require that a multiple of the 8% capital requirement be held.

Federal banking regulators use the Basel Accords as the basis for their capital requirements. Table 4 sets out the specific standards imposed by each.

Table 3. The Basel Accords: Risk Weightings for Selected Financial Assets Under the Standardized Approach (percentages of the 8% baseline capital requirement)

Asset	AAA to AA-	A+ to A-	BBB+ to BBB-	BB+ to B-	Below B-	Unrated
Sovereign Debt	0%	20%	50%	100%	150%	100%
Bank Debt	20%	50%	50%	100%	150%	100%
Corporate Debt	20%	50%	100%	NA	150% (below BB-)	100%
Assets not Assigned Ratings by Standard & Poor's or other Credit Rating Agencies						
Residential Mortgages	35%					
Commercial Real Estate	100%					
Past Due Loans	100%-150% (depending on specific provisions made to cover loan losses)					
Securitization Tranches rated between BB+ and BB- 350%						

Source: Basel Committee on Banking Supervision, International Convergence of Capital Measurement and Capital Standards, BIS, November 2005, pp. 15-22.

Table 4. Capital Standards for Federally Regulated Depository Institutions

Agency	Capital Standard	Source
OCC	Minimum risk-based capital ratio of 8%. (The ratio measures bank capital against assets, with asset values risk-weighted, or adjusted on a scale of riskiness.)	12 CFR § 3.6 ("Minimum capital ratios")
	In addition, banks must maintain Tier 1 capital[a] in an amount equal to at least 3.0% of adjusted total assets. (A simple definition of Tier 1 capital is stockholders' equity, or the net worth of the institution.) The 3% total assets leverage ratio applies to the most highly rated banks, which are expected to have well-diversified risks, including no undue interest rate risk exposure; excellent control systems; good earnings; high asset quality; high liquidity; and well managed on-and off-balance sheet activities; and in general be considered strong banking organiza-tions, with a rating of 1 under CAMELS[b] rating system of banks. For other banks, the minimum Tier 1 leverage ratio is 4%.	

Table 4. (Continued)

Agency	Capital Standard	Source
FDIC	The FDIC requires institutions to maintain the same minimum leverage capital requirements (ratio of Tier 1 capital to assets) as the OCC, that is, 3% for the most highly-rated institutions and 4% for others.	12 CFR § 325.3, (“Minimum leverage capital requirement”)
Federal Reserve	State banks that are members of the Federal Reserve System must meet an 8% risk-weighted capital standard, of which at least 4% must be Tier 1 capital (3% for strong banking institutions	12 CFR § 208.4, Regulation H (“Membership
	rated “1” under the CAMELS rating system of banks). In addition, the Fed establishes levels of reserves that depository institutions are required to maintain for the purpose of facilitating the implementation of monetary policy by the Federal Reserve System.	of State Banking Institutions in the Federal Reserve System”) and 12 CFR § 204.9 (Reserve requirements)
	Reserves consist of vault cash (currency) or deposits at the nearest regional Federal Reserve branch, held against the bank’s deposit liabilities, primarily checking, saving, and time deposits (CDs). The size of these reserves places a ceiling on the amount of deposits that financial institutions can have outstanding, and ties deposit liabilities to the amount of assets (loans) these institutions can acquire.	
OTS	Risk-based capital must be at least 8% of risk-weighted assets. Federal statute requires that OTS capital regulations be no less stringent than the OCC’s. Tangible capital must exceed 1.5% of adjusted total assets. The leverage ratio (Tier 1 capital to assets) must be 4% of adjusted total assets (3% for thrifts with a composite CAMELS rating of 1).	12 CFR §567
NCUA	Credit unions must maintain a risk-based net worth of 7%, as a minimum to be considered well-capitalized.	NCUA Regulations (Section 702, Subpart A)

Source: CRS.

a. Tier 1 capital or core capital means the sum of common stockholders’ equity, noncumulative perpetual preferred stock, and minority interests in consolidated subsidiaries, minus all intangible assets, minus identified losses, minus investments in certain financial subsidiaries, and minus the amount of the total adjusted carrying value of nonfinancial equity investments that is subject to a deduction from Tier 1 capital.

b. See Appendix B.

Non-Bank Capital Requirements

The SEC's Net Capital Rule

The SEC's net capital rule, set out in17 CFR 240.15c3-1, imposes an "Aggregate Indebtedness Standard." No broker/dealer shall permit its aggregate indebtedness to all other persons to exceed 1500% of its net capital (or 800% of its net capital for 12 months after commencing business as a broker or dealer). The 1500% (or 15-to-1) ratio of debt to liquid capital, is arithmetically equivalent to a 6 % capital requirement.

To calculate liquid capital, SEC rules require that securities and other assets be given a "haircut" from their current market values (or face value, in the case of bonds), to cover the risk that the asset's value might decline before it could be sold. The haircut concept is essentially the same as the standardized risk weights in the Basel Accords. The riskier the asset, the greater the haircut. For example, U.S. Treasury securities might have a haircut of zero to 1%; municipal securities, 7%; corporate bonds, 15%; common stock, 20%; and certain assets, such as unsecured receivables or securities for which no ready market exists, receive a haircut of 100%. As discussed below, the intent of the net capital rule is not the same as that of banking capital requirements, because the SEC is not a safety and soundness regulator. The net capital rule is meant to ensure that brokerages cease operations while they still have assets to meet their customers' claims.

CFTC Capital Requirements

Futures commission merchants (or FCMs, the futures equivalent of a securities broker/dealer) are subject to adjusted net capital requirements. Authority to enforce the capital rules is delegated by the CFTC to the National Futures Association (NFA), a self-regulatory organization created by Congress.

Each NFA Member that is required to be registered with the CFTC as a Futures Commission Merchant (Member FCM) must maintain "Adjusted Net Capital" (as defined in CFTC Regulation 1.17) equal to or in excess of the greatest of:

(i) $500,000;
(ii) For Member FCMs with less than $2,000,000 in Adjusted Net Capital, $6,000 for each remote location operated;
(iii) For Member FCMs with less than $2,000,000 in Adjusted Net Capital, $3,000 for each associated person;

(iv) For securities brokers and dealers, the amount of net capital specified by SEC regulations;

(v) 8% of domestic and foreign domiciled customer and 4% of non-customer (excluding proprietary) risk maintenance margin/ performance bond requirements for all domestic and foreign futures and options on futures contracts excluding the risk margin associated with naked long option positions;

(vi) For Member FCMs with an affiliate that engages in foreign exchange (FX) transactions and that is authorized to engage in those transactions solely by virtue of its affiliation with a registered FCM, $7,500,000; or

(vii)For Member FCMs that are counterparties to FX options, $5,000,000, except that FX Dealer Members must meet the higher requirement in Financial Requirements Section 11.[7]

Federal Housing Finance Agency

FHFA is authorized to set capital classification standards for the Federal Home Loan Banks, Fannie Mae, and Freddie Mac that reflect the differences in operations between the banks and the latter two gocerbment-sponsored enterprises.[8] The law defines several capital classifications, and prescribes regulatory actions to be taken as a GSE's condition worsens.

FHFA may downgrade the capital classification of a regulated entity (1) whose conduct could rapidly deplete core or total capital, or (in the case of Fannie or Freddie) whose mortgage assets have declined significantly in value, (2) which is determined (after notice and opportunity for a hearing) to be in an unsafe or unsound condition, or (3) which is engaging in an unsafe or unsound practice.

No growth in total assets is permitted for an *undercapitalized* GSE, unless (1) FHFA has accepted the GSE's capital restoration plan, (2) an increase in assets is consistent with the plan, and (3) the ratio of both total capital to assets and tangible equity to assets is increasing. An undercapitalized entity is subject to heightened scrutiny and supervision.

If a regulated entity is *significantly undercapitalized*, FHFA must take one or more of the following actions: new election of Directors, dismissal of Directors and/or executives, and hiring of qualified executive officers, or other actions. Without prior written approval, executives of a significantly undercapitalized regulated entity may not receive bonuses or pay raises. In addition, FHFA may appoint a receiver or conservator for several specified causes related to financial difficulty and/or violations of law or regulation.

When a GSE becomes *critically undercapitalized*, mandatory receivership or conservatorship provisions apply. For example, FHFA must appoint itself as the receiver if a regulated entity's assets are (and have been for 60 days) less than its obligations to its creditors, or if the regulated entity has (for 60 days) not been generally paying its debts as they come due. The FHFA appointed itself conservator for both Fannie and Freddie in September 2008, before either GSE had failed to make timely payments on debt obligations.

THE FEDERAL FINANCIAL REGULATORS

Banking Regulators

Banking regulation in United States has evolved over time into a system of multiple regulators with overlapping jurisdictions. There is a dual banking system, in which each depository institution is subject to regulation by its chartering authority: state or federal. In addition, because virtually all depository institutions are federally insured, they are subject to at least one federal primary regulator (i.e., the federal authority responsible for examining the institution for safety and soundness and for ensuring its compliance with federal banking laws). The primary federal regulator of national banks is their chartering authority, the Office of the Comptroller of the Currency (OCC). The primary federal regulator of state-chartered banks that are members of the Federal Reserve System is the Board of Governors of the Federal Reserve System. State-chartered banks that are not members of the Federal Reserve System have the FDIC as their primary federal regulator. Thrifts (both state- or federally chartered) have the Office of Thrift Supervision as their primary federal regulator. All of these, because their deposits are covered by FDIC deposit insurance, are also subject to FDIC's regulatory authority. Credit unions–federally chartered or federally insured–are regulated by the National Credit Union Administration. Federal consumer protection laws, many of which are implemented under rules issued by the Board of Governors of the Federal Reserve System, are enforced upon depository institutions by their primary federal regulator.

In general, lenders are expected to be prudent when extending loans. Each loan creates risk for the lender. The overall portfolio of loans extended or held by a lender, in relation to other assets and liabilities, affects that institution's stability. The relationship of lenders to each other, and to wider financial markets, affects the financial system's stability. The nature of these risks can vary between industry sectors, including commercial loans, farm loans, and consumer loans. Safety and soundness regulation encompasses the characteristics of (1) each loan, (2) the balance sheet of each institution, and (3) the risks in the system as a whole.

Each loan has a variety of risk characteristics of concern to lenders and their regulators. Some of these risk characteristics can be estimated at the time the loan is issued. Credit risk, for example, is the risk that the borrower will fail to repay the principal of the loan as promised. Rising interest rates create another risk because the shorter-term interest rates that the lender often pays for its funds rise (e.g., deposit or CD rates) while the longer-term interest rates that the lender will receive from fixed-rate borrowers remain unchanged. Falling interest rates are not riskless either: fixed-rate borrowers may choose to repay loans early, reducing the lender's expected future cash flow. Federal financial regulators take into account expected default rates, prepayment rates, interest-rate exposure, and other risks when examining the loans issued by covered lenders.

Each lender's balance sheet can reduce or enhance the risks of the individual loans that make it up. A lender with many loans exposed to prepayment risk when interest rates fall, for example, could compensate by acquiring some assets that rise in value when interest rates fall. One example of a compensating asset would be an interest-rate derivative contract. Lenders are required to keep capital in reserve against the possibility of a drop in value of loan portfolios or other risky assets. Federal financial regulators take into account compensating assets, risk-based capital requirements, and other prudential standards when examining the balance sheets of covered lenders.

When regulators determine that a bank is taking excessive risks, or engaging in unsafe and unsound practices, they have a number of powerful tools at their disposal to reduce risk to the institution (and ultimately to the federal deposit insurance fund). They can require banks to reduce specified lending or financing practices, dispose of certain assets, and order banks to take steps to restore sound balance sheets. Banks have no alternative but to comply, since regulators have life-or-death options, such as withdrawing deposit insurance or seizing the bank outright.

The five federal banking agencies are briefly discussed below.

Office of the Comptroller of the Currency

The Office of the Comptroller of the Currency (OCC) was created in 1863 as part of the Department of Treasury to supervise federally chartered banks ("national" banks) and to replace the circulation of state bank notes with a single national currency (Chapter 106, 13 STAT. 99). The OCC regulates a wide variety of financial functions, but only for federally chartered banks. The head of the OCC, the Comptroller, is also a member of the board of the FDIC and a director of the Neighborhood Reinvestment Corporation. The OCC has examination powers to enforce its responsibilities for the safety and soundness of nationally chartered banks. The OCC has strong enforcement powers, including the ability to issue cease and desist orders and revoke federal bank charters.

In addition to institution-level examinations, the OCC oversees systemic risk among nationally chartered banks. The OCC's use of the term systemic risk is more consistent with the linkages definition than the undiversifiable risk definition. One example of OCC systemic concerns is the regular survey of credit underwriting practices. This survey compares underwriting standards over time and assesses whether OCC examiners believe the credit risk of nationally chartered bank portfolios is rising or falling. In addition, the OCC publishes regular reports on the derivatives activities of U.S. commercial banks.

Federal Deposit Insurance Corporation

The Federal Deposit Insurance Corporation (FDIC) was created in 1933 to provide assurance to small depositors that they would not lose their savings if their bank failed (P.L. 74-305, 49 Stat. 684). The FDIC is an independent agency that insures deposits, examines and supervises financial institutions, and manages receiverships, assuming and disposing of the assets of failed banks. The FDIC manages the deposit insurance fund, which consists of risk-based assessments levied on depository institutions. The fund is used for various purposes, primarily for resolving failed or failing institutions. The FDIC has broad jurisdiction because nearly all banks and thrifts, whether federally or state-chartered, carry FDIC insurance.

Deposit insurance reform was enacted in 2006 (P.L. 109-173, 119 STAT. 3601), including raising the coverage limit for retirement accounts to $250,000 and indexing both its limit and the general deposit insurance coverage ceiling to inflation. The reform act made changes to the risk-based assessment system to determine the payments of individual institutions. Within a range set by the reform act, the FDIC uses notice and comment rulemaking to set the designated reserve ratio (DRR) that supports the Deposit Insurance Fund (DIF). The FDIC uses its power to examine individual institutions and to issue regulations for all insured depository institutions to monitor and enforce safety and soundness.

In 2008, as the financial crisis worsened, Congress enacted a temporary increase in the deposit insurance ceiling from $100,000 to $250,000 for most accounts.[9] Using emergency authority it received under the Federal Deposit Insurance Corporation Improvement Act of 1991 (FDICIA, P.L. 102-242),[10] the FDIC made a determination of systemic risk in October 2008 and announced that it would temporarily guarantee (1) newly issued senior unsecured debt of banks, thrifts, and certain holding companies, and (2) non-interest bearing deposit transaction accounts (e.g., business checking accounts), regardless of dollar amount.[11]

The Federal Reserve

The Board of Governors of the Federal Reserve System was established in 1913 to provide stability in the banking sector through the regulation of bank reserves (P.L. 63-43, 38 STAT. 251). The System consists of the Board of Governors in Washington and 12 regional reserve banks. In addition to its authority to conduct national monetary policy, the Federal Reserve has safety and soundness examination authority for a variety of lending institutions including bank holding companies; U.S. branches of foreign banks; and state-chartered banks that are members of the federal reserve system. Under the Gramm-Leach-Bliley Act (GLBA, P.L. 106-102), the Fed serves as the umbrella regulator for financial holding companies, which are defined as conglomerates that are permitted to engage in a broad array of financially related activities.

In addition to institution-level examinations of covered lenders, the Federal Reserve oversees systemic risk. This role has come about not entirely through deliberate policy choices, but partly by default, as a result of the Fed's position as lender of last resort and its consequent ability to inject capital or liquidity into troubled institutions. The Federal Reserve's standard response to a financial crisis has been to announce that it stood ready to provide liquidity to the system. This announcement worked well until 2007: a range of crises—the Penn Central bankruptcy, the stock market crash of 1987, the junk bond collapse, sovereign debt crises, the Asian crises of 1997-1998, the dot.com crash, and the 9/11 attacks—were quickly brought under control without systemic consequences. In 2007, however, the Fed's liquidity provision failed to restore stability. As a result, the Fed's role as the primary systemic risk regulator will be closely scrutinized.

Office of Thrift Supervision

The Office of Thrift Supervision (OTS), created in 1989 during the savings and loan crisis (P.L. 101-73, 103 STAT. 183), is the successor institution to the Federal Savings and Loan Insurance Corporation (FSLIC), created in 1934 and administered by the old Federal Home Loan Bank Board. The OTS has the responsibility of monitoring the safety and soundness of federal savings associations and their holding companies. The OTS also supervises federally insured state savings associations. The OTS is part of the Treasury Department but is primarily funded by assessments on covered institutions. The primary business model of most thrifts is accepting deposits and offering home loans, but thrifts offer many other financial services.

There are three main advantages for firms to choose a federal thrift charter. First, a federal thrift charter shields the institution from some state regulations, because federal banking law can preempt state law.[12] Second, a federal thrift charter permits the institution to open branches nationwide under a single regulator, while state-chartered thrifts must comply with multiple state regulators. Third, a federal thrift charter and its holding company are regulated by the same regulator, but a federal bank charter may split regulation of the institution (OCC) from regulation of its holding company (FRB). Thus, a number of diversified financial institutions that are not primarily savings and loans have come under the supervision of OTS as "thrift holding companies," including Lehman Brothers, AIG, and Morgan Stanley.

OTS was created in response to the savings and loan crisis of the late 1980s. That crisis was characterized by an increase in the number of bad loans coincident with inflation, rising costs of deposits, and significantly declining collateral values, primarily in commercial real estate. The magnitude of the losses threatened to overwhelm the deposit insurance funds in the FSLIC. In 1989 Congress enacted the Financial Institutions Reform, Recovery, and Enforcement Act of 1989 (FIRREA, P.L. 101-73), which reorganized thrift regulation and created OTS. FIRREA also created the Resolution Trust Corporation (RTC), charged with sorting out which thrifts could be successfully reorganized or merged with others and which were beyond help. The RTC paid deposit insurance claims and liquidated the assets of failed thrifts.

National Credit Union Administration

The National Credit Union Administration (NCUA), originally part of the Farm Credit Administration, became an independent agency in 1970 (P.L. 91-206, 84 STAT. 49). The NCUA regulates all federal credit unions and those state credit unions that elect to be federally insured. It administers a Central Liquidity Facility, which is the credit union lender of last resort, and the National Credit Union Share Insurance Fund, which insures credit union deposits. Credit unions are member-owned financial cooperatives, and must be not-for-profit institutions. As such, they receive preferential tax treatment compared to mid-sized banks.

Non-Bank Financial Regulators

Securities and Exchange Commission

The Securities and Exchange Commission (SEC) was created as an independent agency in 1934 to enforce newly-written federal securities laws (P.L. 73-291, 48 Stat. 881). The SEC is not primarily concerned with ensuring the safety and soundness of the firms it regulates, but rather with maintaining fair and orderly markets and protecting investors from fraud. This distinction largely arises from the absence of government guarantees for securities investors comparable to deposit insurance. The SEC does not have the authority to limit risks taken by non-bank financial institutions, nor the ability to prop up a failing firm. Two types of firms come under the SEC's jurisdiction: (1) all corporations that sell securities to the public, and (2) securities broker/dealers and other securities markets intermediaries.

Firms that sell securities—stocks and bonds—to the public are required to register with the SEC. Registration entails the publication of detailed information about the firm, its management, the intended uses for the funds raised through the sale of securities, and the risks to investors. The initial registration disclosures must be kept current through the filing of periodic financial statements: annual and quarterly reports (as well as special reports when there is a material change in the firm's financial condition or prospects).

Beyond these disclosure requirements, and certain other rules that apply to corporate governance, the SEC does not have any direct regulatory control over publicly traded firms. Bank regulators are expected to identify unsafe and unsound banking practices in the institutions they supervise, and have power to intervene and prevent banks from taking excessive risks. The SEC has no comparable authority; the securities laws simply require that risks be disclosed to investors. Registration with the SEC, in other words, is in no sense a guarantee that a security is a good or safe investment.

To enable investors to make informed investment choices, the SEC has statutory authority over financial accounting standards. All publicly traded firms are required to use generally accepted accounting principles (GAAP), which are formulated by the Financial Accounting Standards Board (FASB), the American Institute of Certified Public Accountants (AICPA), and the SEC itself.

Besides publicly traded corporations, a number of securities market participants are also required to register with the SEC (or with one of the industry self-regulatory organizations that the SEC oversees). These include stock exchanges, securities brokerages (and numerous classes of their personnel), mutual funds, auditors, investment advisers, and others. To maintain their registered status, all these entities must comply with rules meant to protect public investors, prevent fraud, and promote fair and orderly markets. The area of SEC supervision most analogous to banking regulation is broker/dealer regulation. Several provisions of law and regulation protect brokerage customers from losses arising from brokerage firm failure. The Securities Investor Protection Corporation (SIPC), created by Congress in 1970, operates an insurance scheme funded by assessments on broker/dealers (and with a backup line of credit with the U.S. Treasury). SIPC guarantees customer accounts up to $500,000 for losses arising from brokerage failure or fraud (but not market losses). Unlike the FDIC, however, SIPC does not examine broker/dealers and has no regulatory powers.

Since 1975, the SEC has enforced a net capital rule applicable to all registered broker/dealers. The rule requires broker/dealers to maintain an excess of capital above mere solvency, to ensure that a failing firm stops trading while it still has assets to meet customer claims. Net capital levels are calculated in a manner similar to the risk-based capital requirements under the Basel Accords, but the SEC has its own set of risk weightings, which it calls haircuts. The riskier the asset, the greater the haircut.

While the net capital rule appears to be very close in its effects to the banking agencies' risk-based capital requirements, there are significant differences. The SEC has no authority to intervene in a broker/dealer's business if it takes excessive risks that might cause net capital to drop below the required level. Rather, the net capital rule is often described as a liquidation rule—not meant to prevent failures but to minimize the impact on customers. Moreover, the SEC has no authority comparable to the banking regulators' prompt corrective action powers: it cannot preemptively seize a troubled broker/dealer or compel it to merge with a sound firm.

The differences between bank and securities regulation with respect to safety and soundness came into sharp focus with the collapse of Bear Stearns, one of the five largest investment banks, in March 2008.[13] The SEC monitored

Bear Stearns' financial condition until shortly before the collapse (which was precipitated by the refusal of other market participants to extend short-term credit), and believed that the firm had sufficient levels of capital and liquidity. When bankruptcy suddenly loomed, it was the Federal Reserve that stepped in to broker the sale of Bear Stearns to JP Morgan Chase by agreeing to purchase $30 billion of "toxic" Bear Stearns assets.

The Bear Stearns situation highlighted several apparent anomalies in the U.S. regulatory structure. The SEC lacked safety and soundness powers over the institutions it supervised, while the Fed was forced to commit funds to an investment bank over which it had no regulatory jurisdiction. The anomaly became even more pronounced when the Fed subsequently established a lending facility to provide short-term credit to other investment banks.[14]

The Bear Stearns collapse showed the inability of the SEC to respond to a brokerage failure with systemic risk implications. There is more to the story, however, than the differences between bank regulation and the SEC's net capital rule. In 2004, the SEC devised a voluntary supervisory scheme for the largest investment banks, called the Consolidated Supervised Entities (CSE) program.[15] The CSE firms were all registered broker/dealers, but were also large holding companies with extensive operations carried on outside the broker/dealer unit. Thus, the SEC had no capital requirement that applied to the entire investment bank. Under CSE, this was to change: as a substitute for the net capital rule, the firms agreed to abide by the Basel risk-based standard, and maintain that level of capital *at the holding company level.* On a voluntary basis, the firms agreed to grant the SEC the authority to examine and monitor their compliance, above and beyond the SEC's explicit statutory authority.[16]

Whatever the intent of the CSE program, it did not succeed in preventing excessive risk-taking by the participants.[17] By the end of September 2008, all five CSE investment banks had either failed (Lehman Brothers), merged to prevent failure (Merrill Lynch and Bear Stearns), or applied for bank holding company status (Morgan Stanley and Goldman Sachs).[18] On September 26, 2008, SEC Chairman Cox announced the end of the CSE program, declaring that "[t]he last six months have made it abundantly clear that voluntary regulation does not work. When Congress passed the Gramm-Leach-Bliley Act, it created a significant regulatory gap by failing to give to the SEC or any agency the authority to regulate large investment bank holding companies."[19]

Commodity Futures Trading Commission

The Commodity Futures Trading Commission (CFTC) was created in 1974 to regulate commodities futures and options markets, which at the time were poised to expand beyond their traditional base in agricultural commodities to encompass contracts based on financial variables such as interest rates and stock indexes. The CFTC's mission is to prevent excessive speculation, manipulation of commodity prices, and fraud. Like the SEC, the CFTC oversees industry self-regulatory organizations (SROs)—the futures exchanges and the National Futures Association—and requires the registration of a range of industry firms and personnel, including futures commission merchants (brokers), floor traders, commodity pool operators, and commodity trading advisers.

Like the SEC, the CFTC does not directly regulate the safety and soundness of individual firms. Nevertheless, its oversight can have important consequences for the ability of market participants to manage financial risk. Futures, options, and derivatives can have a systemic impact.

Some argue that the CFTC's ability to respond to systemic crises is limited because a large part of the derivatives market is exempt from its jurisdiction. Derivatives contracts may be traded in an unregulated over-the-counter (OTC) market, so long as no small investors are allowed to trade. OTC derivatives are some of the largest financial markets in the world, and many OTC market participants also trade on the CFTC-regulated futures exchanges, but the CFTC does not receive regular reports about price, volume, and size of positions in the OTC markets.

Federal Housing Finance Agency

The Federal Housing Finance Agency (FHFA) was created in 2008 by the Housing and Economic Recovery Act of 2008 (P.L. 110-289) to consolidate and strengthen regulation of a group of housing finance-related government-sponsored enterprises (GSEs): Fannie Mae, Freddie Mac, and the Federal Home Loan Banks.[20] The FHFA succeeded the Office of Federal Housing Enterprise Oversight (OFHEO) and the Federal Housing Finance Board (FHFB).

The impetus to create the FHFA came from concerns about risk—including systemic risk—arising from the rapid growth of the GSEs, particularly Fannie and Freddie. These two GSEs were profit-seeking, shareholder-owned corporations that took advantage of their government-sponsored status to accumulate undiversified investment portfolios of over $1.5 trillion, consisting almost exclusively of home mortgages (and securities and derivatives based on those mortgages).

The FHFA was given enhanced safety and soundness powers resembling those of the federal bank regulators. These powers included the ability to set capital standards, to order the enterprises to cease any activity or divest any asset that posed a threat to financial soundness, and to replace management and assume control of the firms if they became seriously undercapitalized.

The FHFA's first action was to place both Fannie and Freddie in conservatorship.[21] Fannie and Freddie continue to operate, under an agreement with the U.S. Treasury. The Treasury will provide capital to the two firms, by means of preferred stock purchases, to ensure that each remains solvent. In return, the government assumed a 79.9% equity ownership position in the firms.

Regulatory Umbrella Groups

The need for coordination and data sharing among regulators has led to the formation of innumerable interagency task forces to study particular market episodes and make recommendations to Congress. Two interagency organizations have attained permanent status.

Federal Financial Institution Examinations Council

The Federal Financial Institutions Examination Council (FFIEC) was created by legislation[22] in 1979 as a formal interagency body to coordinate federal regulation of lending institutions. Through the FFIEC, the federal banking regulators issue a single set of reporting forms for covered institutions. The FFIEC also attempts to harmonize auditing principles and supervisory decisions. The FFIEC is made up of the Federal Reserve, OCC, FDIC, OTS, and NCUA, each of which employs examiners to enforce safety and soundness regulations for lending institutions.

- Federal financial institution examiners evaluate the risks of covered institutions. The specific safety and soundness concerns common to the FFIEC agencies can be found in the handbooks employed by examiners to monitor lenders. Each subject area of the handbook can be updated separately. Examples of safety and soundness subject areas include important indicators of risk, such as capital adequacy, asset quality, liquidity, and sensitivity to market risk.

President's Working Group on Financial Markets

The President's Working Group on Financial Markets (PWG) was created by President Reagan through executive order in 1988.[23] The PWG includes the Secretary of the Treasury and the Chairmen of the Federal Reserve, the SEC, and the CFTC. It is not a formal agency subject to congressional oversight, although each member is subject to Senate confirmation at the time of appointment.

The impetus for the creation of the PWG was the stock market crash of October 1987, and specifically the role that the stock index futures markets (under CFTC jurisdiction) had played in creating panic in the stock market (regulated by SEC). Studies conducted by the SEC, the CFTC, a blue-ribbon panel appointed by the President (the Presidential Task Force on Market Mechanisms, or Brady Commission), and the stock and futures exchanges reached strikingly different conclusions; the task of the PWG was to study the studies and issue a further report.

The PWG was not dissolved, but continued to provide interagency coordination and information sharing, and to study entities and products that raised intermarket regulatory issues, such as hedge funds and OTC derivatives. In March 2008, at the direction of President Bush, the PWG issued a policy statement on the ongoing financial crisis.[24]

Unregulated Markets and Institutions

Although federal financial statutes and regulations fill many volumes, not all participants in the financial system are regulated. In some cases, unregulated (or self-regulated) markets appear to work very well, but disruptions or major frauds in these markets are likely to bring calls for increased government supervision. The dynamic nature of financial markets is a perennial challenge to regulatory structure design, because a market that appears insignificant at the time a law is written may grow into a potential threat to systemic stability in a few years. The following are some of the major unregulated markets and institutions.

Foreign Exchange Markets

Buying and selling currencies is essential to foreign trade, and the exchange rate determined by traders has major implications for a country's macroeconomic policy. The market is one of the largest in the world, with daily turnover in excess of $3 trillion.[25] Nevertheless, no U.S. agency has regulatory authority over the foreign exchange market.

Trading in currencies takes place between large global banks, central banks, hedge funds and other currency speculators, commercial firms involved in imports and exports, fund managers, and retail brokers. There is no centralized marketplace, but rather a number of proprietary electronic platforms that have largely supplanted the traditional telephone broker market.

Despite the fact that extreme volatility in exchange rates for a number of European and Asian currencies in the 1990s was often blamed on currency speculators, neither U.S. nor foreign regulators have moved towards regulating the market.

U.S. Treasury Securities

The secondary, or resale, market for Treasury securities is largely unregulated. Like the foreign exchange market, there is no central exchange, but there are a number of proprietary, computer-based transaction systems. Treasury securities were exempted from SEC regulation by the original securities laws of the 1930s. In 1993, following a successful corner of a Treasury bond auction by Salomon Brothers, Congress passed the Government Securities Act Amendments (P.L. 103-202), which required brokers and dealers that were not already registered with the SEC to register as government securities dealers. (Existing broker/dealer registrants were simply required to notify the SEC that they were in the government securities business.) Nevertheless, the government securities market remains much more lightly regulated than the corporate securities markets.

The primary market in Treasury securities, where new debt instruments are sold to fund government operations, is also relatively unregulated. A principal channel for the distribution of new Treasuries is a group of firms called primary dealers, who purchase securities at auction for their own accounts and for their customers. The primary dealers are 19 commercial and investment banks, both foreign and domestic. The primary dealer list is maintained by the Federal Reserve Bank of New York, which conducts auctions for the Treasury, but its relationship to the dealers is commercial, rather than regulatory.[26] The New York Fed does, however, collect certain data about primary dealers' transactions in government securities.

In March 2008, as part of its multifaceted attempt to supply liquidity to the financial system, the Federal Reserve established a Primary Dealer Credit Facility, to make short-term loans against a variety of collateral (including asset-backed and mortgage-backed securities) to the primary dealers.[27] This step attracted attention because the primary dealer group included investment banking firms over which the Fed had no regulatory authority.

OTC Derivatives

As noted above, the Commodity Exchange Act contains exemptions from CFTC regulation for derivative contracts and markets where all traders are "eligible contract participants," that is, not small businesses or retail investors. About two-thirds of OTC derivatives are contracts linked to interest rates; foreign exchange and credit derivatives each account for about 9%; and contracts linked to physical commodity and stock prices account for about 2% each.[28]

Whether the unregulated status of OTC derivatives constitutes a troublesome regulatory gap has been debated in Congress and among the regulators. One view has been that there is no government interest in regulating these markets, since all participants are sophisticated and able to manage the risks. Another is that derivatives contracts make up an invisible web of financial obligations and exposures, and that the failure of a large derivatives dealer could trigger cascading losses throughout the global system.

A case that is likely to shape debate is that of AIG, whose insurance operations are regulated by New York state, but whose large derivatives trading business—the firm was a leader in the credit default swap market[29]—was not regulated (although, technically, the firm was a thrift holding company under OTS supervision). Massive losses in credit default swaps forced the Fed and Treasury to craft an ad hoc rescue of AIG, which involves over $150 billion in loans and guarantees.[30]

Private Securities Markets

The securities laws mandate registration of and extensive disclosures by public securities issuers, but also provide for private sales of securities, which are not subject to disclosure requirements. Private placements of securities may only be offered to limited numbers of "accredited investors" who meet certain asset tests. (Most purchasers are life insurers and other institutional investors.) There are also restrictions on the resale of private securities.

The size of the private placement market is subject to considerable variation from year to year, but at times the value of securities sold privately exceeds what is sold into the public market. In recent decades, venture capitalists and private equity firms have come to play important roles in corporate finance. The former typically purchase interests in private firms, which may be sold later to the public, while the latter often purchase all the stock of publicly traded companies and take them private.

Nonbank Lenders

During the housing boom of the early 2000s, substantial volumes of mortgages were written not by chartered depository institutions, but by nonbank lenders with access to credit from Wall Street firms involved in the securitization of mortgages. These lenders were not subject to safety and soundness regulation, although they were required to comply with the Federal Reserve's Truth in Lending Act consumer protection regulations. Many view these lenders as having been instrumental in the relaxation of credit standards, leading to what many now regard as the unsustainable housing price bubble that triggered the current crisis.[31]

Hundreds of these nonbank mortgage lenders failed in 2007 and 2008, as delinquency rates on their subprime and other non-traditional mortgages soared. Potential reforms of securitization and the non-bank lending channel are now under consideration.[32]

Hedge Funds

Hedge funds are pools of managed money that structure themselves to fit into exemptions in the federal securities laws—in effect, they are unregulated mutual funds. By limiting the number of investors, and restricting access to wealthy investors who meet specified asset tests, hedge funds avoid regulation by the SEC.[33] Since there are no reporting requirements, the size of the hedge fund universe can only be estimated, but before losses in 2008, it was commonly stated that hedge funds had about $2 trillion of investor funds under management.

Hedge funds have shown their potential for causing systemic disturbances. The case of Long Term Capital Management (LTCM) is one example of the Federal Reserve arranging for reorganization of an institution believed to pose systemic risk if it failed. Another hedge fund debacle—the failure of the Amaranth fund—is said to have caused significant fluctuations in the price of natural gas.[34] It is noteworthy, however, that hedge fund failures do not appear to have played a major role in the development of the current financial crisis. Some have argued that they may actually have played a stabilizing role, by absorbing losses that would otherwise have accrued to regulated financial institutions. But this judgment is regarded by others as premature; the crisis continues to unfold.

Comprehensive Reform Legislation in the 111th Congress

Although there have been many bills introduced in the 111th Congress that could affect financial regulation, two comprehensive measures have been addressed by committees of jurisdiction. The House has aggregated a number of financial reform proposals into H.R. 4173, the "Wall Street Reform and Consumer Protection Act of 2009." In the Senate, Chairman Dodd of the Senate Banking, Housing, and Urban Affairs Committee issued a single comprehensive committee print on November 16, 2009. Members of the committee are reportedly pairing up to revise Senator Dodd's discussion draft in a bipartisan fashion. The major topics of these bills follow the general outline of Treasury's proposal that was issued in a series of titles released during the summer of 2009.

Both the House and the Senate bills would reorganize the authorities of some financial regulators. For example, both bills would remove consumer protection authority from existing financial regulators and place it all in a single new agency dedicated to consumer financial protection. Both bills would remove exemptions for financial derivatives and extend CFTC and SEC authority over more derivatives transactions. Both bills would create a systemic risk council with authority to identify systemically risky firms, gather market information, and monitor concentrations of risk in the financial system. Both bills provide authorities with enhanced resolution authority; a failing systemically important firm would not go through traditional bankruptcy if the systemic risk authorities believe it would cause financial instability. Both bills would reduce the number of banking regulators with examination authority. Both bills provide for more information to be made available to investors and consumers in the marketplace.

There are some significant differences between the two approaches. While the Dodd Committee Print creates a single bank regulatory authority, H.R. 4173 only merges two of the bank regulators (the OCC and OTS). H.R. 4173 would allow the systemic risk regulator to preemptively require it to dispose of assets, or even break it up, if there were concerns about financial stability. The Dodd Committee Print allows for enhanced resolution of failing firms but not for pre-emptive intervention for solvent firms.

The House passed H.R. 4173, the Wall Street Reform and Consumer Protection Act of 2009 on December 11, 2009. The bill included provisions to create a council to address systemic risk, grant regulators enhanced authority to resolve failing systemically important firms, require more derivatives to be cleared through regulated organizations, create an agency focused solely on consumer financial protection, and register some activities of hedge funds. Also, H.R. 4173 was amended to include a revised version of H.R. 1728, the Mortgage Reform and Anti-Predatory Lending Act, which had previously passed the House on May 7, 2009. H.R. 1728 establishes regulatory standards that will apply to all mortgage loans.

Appendix A. Forms of Banking Organizations

The structure of banks can be complex. Currently, the regulator of a particular activity of a bank or its subsidiary in part depends on the activity of the subsidiary or its charter, as described above. The following flow charts provide simplified representations of various bank structures. In some cases, the umbrella bank and its subsidiaries may have different regulators.

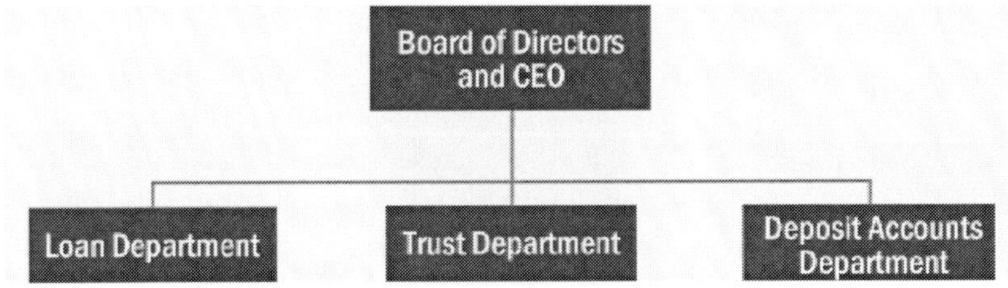

Figure A-1. National Bank

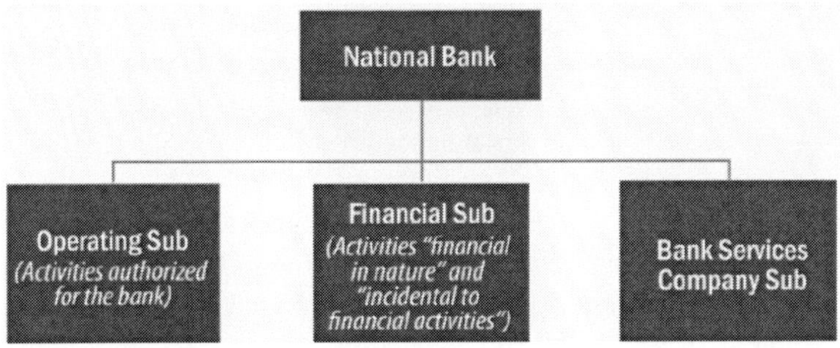

Figure A-2. National Bank and Subsidiaries

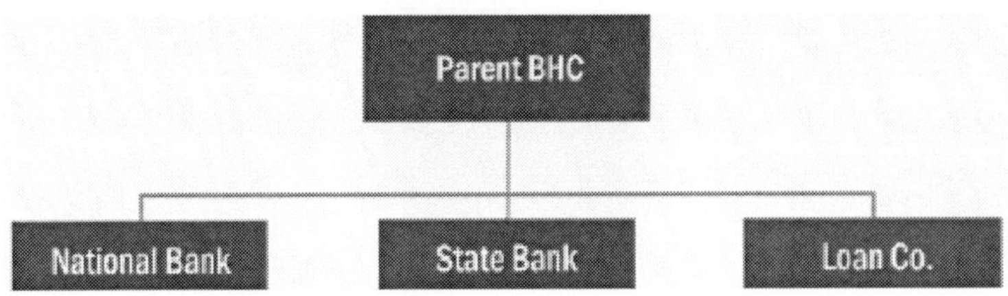

Figure A-3. Bank Holding Company

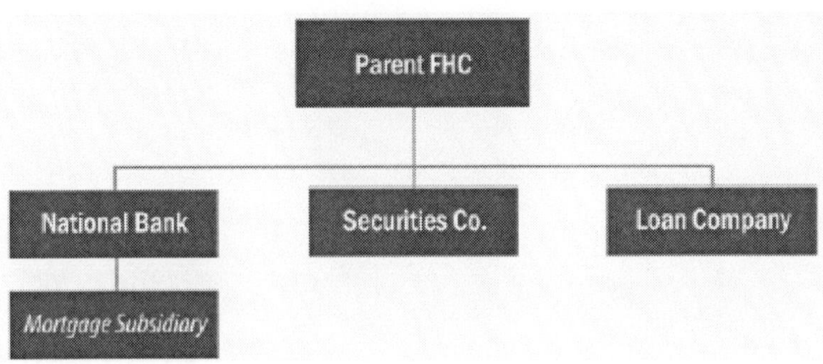

Figure A-4. Financial Holding Company

APPENDIX B. BANK RATINGS: UFIRS AND CAMELS

Federal bank regulators conduct confidential assessments of covered banks. The Federal Financial Institutions Examination Council (FFIEC) helps coordinate the ratings system used by bank examiners so that there is some consistency to the examinations, although the ratings do take into account differences in bank size, sophistication, complexity of activities, and risk profile. The FFIEC adopted the Uniform Financial Institutions Rating System (UFIRS) in 1979. The system was revised in 1996 and is often referred to as the CAMELS rating system. CAMELS stands for Capital adequacy, Asset quality, Management, Earnings, Liquidity, and Sensitivity to market risk. A description of the CAMELS system is found in the Comptrollers Handbook: Bank Supervision Process, provided by the OCC.[35] Market factors can affect more than one category in the CAMELS ratings.

Capital Adequacy

This component assesses the level of capital held by the institution in relation to the risks that it takes. Capital adequacy can be affected by a number of factors, including changes in credit risk, market risk, and the institution's financial condition. Increases in problem assets would require increased capital. Capital adequacy is also supposed to reflect risks even if they are technically off of the bank's balance sheet.

Asset Quality

Asset quality refers to existing and potential credit risk associated with a the bank's portfolio. Like capital adequacy, this component is supposed to reflect risk even if it is not technically on the bank's balance sheet. Asset quality can include changes in loan default rates, investment performance, exposure to counterparty risk, and all other risks that may affect the value or marketability of an institution's assets.

Management Capability

The governance of the bank, including management and board of directors, is assessed in relation to the nature and scope of the bank's activities. This rating is affected by the level and quality of management oversight. It also includes legal compliance, responsiveness to auditor recommendations, and similar issues.

Earnings Quantity and Quality

The rating of a bank's earnings takes into account current earnings and the sustainability of future earnings. Earnings that rely on favorable tax effects and nonrecurring events receive lower ratings. Similarly, inadequate controls for expenses can reduce the rating for earnings. Difficulties in forecasting and managing risks can also reduce the earnings rating.

Liquidity

Liquidity includes the ability of a bank to meet its expected funding needs. For a given institution size and complexity, this factor assesses the ability of the firm to fulfill its financial obligations in a timely manner. Liquidity refers to the ability to meet short-term funding needs without incurring excessive losses, which might occur if assets had to be sold at a steep discount in a time-pressure situation (or "fire sale"). Liquidity also includes assessments of specific financial categories, such as the trend and stability of deposits, and the expected ability to securitize and sell pools of assets.

Sensitivity to Market Risk

Market risk includes potential changes in the prices of financial assets, such as movements in interest rates, foreign exchange rates, commodity prices, and stock prices. The nature and scope of a bank's activities can affect the markets that it is exposed to; therefore, market risk is closely related to the other CAMELS factors. This rating takes into account management's ability to identify and manage the risks that can arise from the bank's trading activities in financial markets. It also takes into account interest rate risk from nontrading positions, such as any duration mismatch in loans held to maturity.

APPENDIX C. ACRONYMS

AICPA	American Institute of Certified Public Accountants
CAMELS	Capital Adequacy, Asset Quality, Management, Liquidity, Sensitivity to Market Risk
CFTC	Commodity Futures Trading Commission
CSE	Consolidated Supervised Entities
EESA	Emergency Economic Stabilization Act
FASB	Financial Accounting Standards Board
FDIC	Federal Deposit Insurance Corporation
FFIEC	Federal Financial Institution Examination Council
FHFA	Federal Housing Finance Agency
FHFB	Federal Housing Finance Board
FRB	Federal Reserve Board
FSLIC	Federal Savings and Loan Insurance Corporation
GAAP	Generally Accepted Accounting Principles
GSE	Government-Sponsored Enterprise
NCUA	National Credit Union Administration
OCC	Office of the Comptroller of the Currency
OFHEO	Office of Federal Housing Enterprise Oversight
OTS	Office of Thrift Supervision
PWG	President's Working Group on Capital Markets
SEC	Securities and Exchange Commission
SIPC	Securities Investor Protection Corporation
SRO	Self Regulatory Organization
UFIRS	Uniform Financial Institutions Rating System

APPENDIX D. GLOSSARY OF TERMS

This glossary has been compiled from several earlier CRS reports, from the CFTC and SIFMA websites, and from other sources.

Affiliate—A corporate relationship of control. Two companies are affiliated when one owns all or a large part of another, or when both are controlled by a third (holding) company (see subsidiary). All subsidiaries are affiliates, but affiliates that are less than 50% controlled are usually not treated as subsidiaries.

Agency relationship—A business relationship of two parties in which one represents the other in transactions with third parties. The agent negotiates on behalf of the party actually at risk, who is known as the "principal." A commission goes to the agent who does not take on the risk of the transaction; the profit or loss goes to the principal.

Asset-backed security—A bond that represents a share in a pool of debt obligations or other assets. The holder is entitled to some part of the repayment flows from the underlying debt. (See "securitization.")

Bank holding company—A business incorporated under state law, which controls through equity ownership ("holds") one or more banks and, often, other affiliates in financial services as allowed by its regulator, the Federal Reserve. On the federal level, these businesses are regulated through the Bank Holding Company Act.

Bank Holding Company Act—The federal statute under which the Federal Reserve regulates bank holding companies and financial holding companies (FHC). Besides the permissible financial activities enumerated in the Gramm-Leach-Bliley Act (P.L. 106-102), the law provides a mechanism between the Federal Reserve and the Department of the Treasury to decide what is an appropriate new financial activity for FHCs.

Blue sky laws—State statutes that govern the offering and selling of securities.

Broker/dealer—An individual or firm that buys and sells securities for itself as well as for customers. Broker/dealers are registered with the Securities and Exchange Commission.

Bubble—Self-reinforcing process in which the price of an asset exceeds its fundamental value for a sustained period, often followed by a rapid price decline. Speculative bubbles are usually associated with a "bandwagon" effect in which speculators rush to buy the commodity (in the case of futures, "to take positions") before the price trend ends, and an even greater rush to sell the commodity (unwind positions) when prices reverse.

Capital requirements—Capital is the owners' stake in an enterprise. It is a critical line of defense when losses occur, both in banking and nonbanking enterprises. Capital requirements help assure that losses that might occur will accrue to the institution incurring them. In the case of banking institutions experiencing problems, capital also serves as a buffer against losses to the federal deposit insurance funds.

Charter conversion - Banking institutions may, with the approval of their regulators, switch their corporate form between: commercial bank or savings institution, National or State charter, and to stockholder ownership from depositor ownership. Various regulatory conditions may encourage switching.

Clearing Organization—An entity through which futures and other derivative transactions are cleared and settled. A clearing organization may be a division or affiliate of a particular exchange, or a freestanding entity. Also called a clearing house, multilateral clearing organization, or clearing association.

Collateralized debt obligation (CDO)—A bond created by the securitization of a pool of asset-backed securities.

Collateralized mortgage obligation (CMO)—A multiclass bond backed by a pool of mortgage pass-through securities or mortgage loans.

Commercial bank—A deposit-taking institution that can make commercial loans, accept checking accounts, and whose deposits are insured by the Federal Deposit Insurance Corporation. National banks are chartered by the Office of the Comptroller of the Currency; state banks, by the individual states.

Commodity Futures Modernization Act of 2000 (CFMA, P.L. 106-554, 114 Stat. 2763)—overhauled the Commodity Exchange Act to create a flexible structure for the regulation of futures and options trading, and established a broad statutory exemption from regulation for OTC derivatives.

Community financial institution—As provided for in the Gramm-Leach-Bliley Act, a member of the Federal Home Loan Bank System whose deposits are insured under the Federal Deposit Insurance Act and which has assets of less than $500 million (calculated according to provisions in the law, and in succeeding years to be adjusted for inflation). Such institutions may become members without meeting requirements with regard to the percentage of total assets that must be in residential mortgage loans and may borrow from the Federal Home Loan Banks for small business and agriculture.

Conservatorship—When an insolvent financial institution is reorganized by a regulator with the intent to restoring it to an ongoing business.

Counterparty—The opposite party in a bilateral agreement, contract, or transaction, such as a swap.

Credit Default Swap (CDS)—A tradeable contract in which one party agrees to pay another if a third party experiences a credit event, such as default on a debt obligation, bankruptcy, or credit rating downgrade.

Credit Risk—The risk that a borrower will fail to repay a loan in full, or that a derivatives counterparty will default.

Credit union—A nonprofit financial cooperative of individuals with one or more common bonds (such as employment, labor union membership, or residence in the same neighborhood). May be state or nationally chartered. Credit unions accept deposits of members' savings and transaction balances in the form of share accounts, pay dividends (interest) on them out of earnings, and primarily provide consumer credit to members. The federal regulator for credit unions is the National Credit Union Administration.

Dealer—An individual or financial firm engaged in the purchase and sale of securities and commodities such as metals, foreign exchange, etc., for its own account and at its own risk as principal (see broker). Commercial banks are typically limited to acting as dealers in specified high-quality debt obligations, such as those of the federal government.

Depository institution—Customarily refers to commercial banks, savings institutions, and credit unions, since traditionally the greater part of their funding has been in the form of deposits. Deposits are a customer's funds placed with an institution according to agreed on terms and conditions and represent a credit to the depositor.

Derivatives—Financial contracts whose value is linked to the price of an underlying commodity or financial variable (such as an interest rate, currency price, or stock index). Ownership of a derivative does not require the holder to actually buy or sell the underlying interest. Derivatives are used by hedgers, who seek to shift risk to others, and speculators, who can profit if they can successfully forecast price trends. Examples include futures contracts, options, and swaps.

Discount window—Figurative term for the Federal Reserve facility for extending credit directly to eligible depository institutions. It may be used to relieve temporary cash shortages at banks and other depository institutions. Borrowers are expected to have tried to borrow elsewhere first and must provide collateral as security for loans. The term derives from the practice whereby bankers would come to a Reserve Bank teller window to obtain credit in the early days of the Federal Reserve System.

Dual banking system—The phrase refers to the fact that banks may be either federally or state-chartered. In the case of state-chartered banks, the state is the primary regulator; for national banks, the Office of the Comptroller of the Currency is the primary regulator.

Electronic fund transfer (EFT) systems—A variety of systems and technologies for transferring funds electronically rather than by paper check.

Exchange—A central marketplace with established rules and regulations where buyers and sellers meet to trade futures and options contracts or securities.

Federal Home Loan Banks—Twelve regional member-owned federally sponsored organizations that extend credit to their member banking institutions, largely to finance mortgages made to homeowners. The 12 FHLBs make up a single government-sponsored enterprise.

Federal safety net—A broad term referring to protection of banking institutions through deposit insurance, discount window credit, other lender of last resort support, and certain forms of regulations to reduce risk. Commercial and industrial companies generally lack any of these cushions against loss.

Financial businesses—In discussions about financial services modernization, usually refers to commercial banks and savings institutions, securities firms, and insurance companies and agents, as contrasted with commercial and industrial firms.

Financial holding company—A holding company form authorized by the Gramm-Leach-Bliley Act that goes beyond the limits a of bank holding company. It can control one or more banks, securities firms, and insurance companies as permitted by law and/or regulation.

Financial institution—An enterprise that uses its funds chiefly to purchase financial assets such as loans and debt securities, as opposed to tangible property. Financial institutions are differentiated by the manner in which they invest their funds: in loans, bonds, stocks, or some combination; as well as by their sources of funds. Depository financial institutions are differentiated in that they may accept deposits which are federally insured against loss to the depositor. Nondepository financial institutions such as life and property/casualty insurance companies, pension funds, and mutual funds obtain funds through other types of receipts, whose values may fluctuate with market conditions.

Financial subsidiary—Under the Gramm-Leach-Bliley Act, both national and state-chartered banks are authorized to form financial subsidiaries to engage in activities that would not otherwise be permitted within the bank itself, subject to certain limits. Besides the permissible financial activities enumerated in P.L. 106-102, the law provides a mechanism between the U.S. Department of the Treasury and the Federal Reserve to decide what is an appropriate new financial activity for a financial subsidiary.

Firewalls—Barriers to the flow of capital, information, management, and other resources among business units owned by a common entity. In case of financial distress of one operation ("fire"), the "walls" are intended to prevent the spread of loss to the other units—especially to banking units. Example: losses in a securities subsidiary of a holding company could not be covered by any of the holding company's bank subsidiaries.

Foreign bank—Banks and their holding companies headquartered in other countries may have a variety of financial operations in the United States: U.S.-chartered subsidiary banks, agencies, branches, and representative offices. Their primary federal regulator is the Federal Reserve, under the International Banking Act of 1978 as amended. States and the Office of the Comptroller of the Currency may also regulate them.

Functional regulation—Regulatory arrangements based on activity ("function") rather than organizational structure. The Gramm-Leach-Bliley Act called for more functional regulation than in the past.

Glass-Steagall Act—Part of the Banking Act of 1933; divided the commercial and investment banking industries. The Gramm-Leach-Bliley Act repealed two sections of the act dealing with the relationship between banks and securities firms.

Government-sponsored enterprise (GSE)—GSEs are private companies with government charters. Government sponsorship typically gives them a funding advantage over purely private competitors, while their charters restrict the kinds of businesses they may conduct.

Gramm-Leach-Bliley Act of 1999—P.L. 106-102, also known as the Financial Services Modernization Act, authorized increased affiliations between banks, securities firms, and insurers. Permitted the establishment of financial holding companies, under the regulation of the Federal Reserve. Also addressed privacy protection for consumers' financial data.

Haircut—In computing the value of assets for purposes of capital, segregation, or margin requirements, a percentage reduction from the stated value (e.g., book value or market value) to account for possible declines in value that may occur before assets can be liquidated.

Hedge funds—Hedge funds are essentially unregulated mutual funds. They are pools of invested money that buy and sell stocks and bonds and many other assets, including precious metals, commodities, foreign currencies, and derivatives (contracts whose prices are derived from those of other financial instruments). Hedge funds are limited to qualified investors with high net worth.

Hedging—Investing with the intention of reducing the impact of adverse movements in interest rates, commodities, or securities prices. Typically, the hedging instrument gains value as the hedged item loses value, and vice versa.

Insolvent—A firm whose liabilities exceed its assets.

Institutional regulation—Regulation that is institution-specific as contrasted with activity-specific (see functional regulation).

Investment bank—A financial intermediary, active in the securities business. Investment banking functions include underwriting (marketing newly registered securities to individual or institutional investors), counseling regarding merger and acquisition proposals, brokerage services, advice on corporate financing, and proprietary trading.

Investment bank holding company—A holding company for securities firms authorized under the Gramm-Leach-Bliley Act. Such holding companies are subject to regulation by the Securities and Exchange Commission.

Issuer—A person or entity (including a company or bank) that offers securities for sale. The issuing of securities, where the proceeds accrue to the issuer, is distinct from the secondary, or resale, market, where securities are traded among investors.

Lender of last resort—Governmental lender that acts as the ultimate source of credit in the financial system. In the United States, the Federal Reserve has this role.

Leverage—The ability to control large dollar amounts of a commodity or security with a comparatively small amount of capital. Leverage can be obtained through borrowing or the use of derivatives.

Limited-purpose bank—Although generally commercial firms may not conduct a banking business, some exceptions exist. Examples: Nonbank banks are banks that either accept deposits or make commercial loans but cannot do both. Such banks grew up through a loophole in law which was closed by the Competitive Equality Banking Act of 1987 (CEBA). Credit card banks conduct credit card operations. Industrial loan companies in a few states may offer restricted banking services.

Liquidity—The ability to trade an asset quickly without significantly affecting its price, or the condition of a market with many buyers and sellers present. Also, the ability of a person or firm to access credit markets.

Liquidity risk—The possibility that the market for normally-liquid assets will suddenly dry up, leaving firms unable to convert assets into cash. Also, the risk that other firms will refuse to extend credit on any terms to a firm that is perceived as distressed.

Market risk—The risk that the price of a tradeable security or asset will decline, resulting in a loss to the holder.

Merchant banker—A European style investment banker concentrating on corporate deals, in which it may invest its own funds.

Money market mutual fund (MMF)—A form of mutual fund that pools funds of individuals and other investors for investment in high-grade, short-term debt and bank deposits paying market rates of return. Examples of these money market instruments include U.S. Treasury bills, certificates of deposit, and commercial paper. In addition to the investment features, most MMFs offer check-writing redemption features.

Moral hazard—The tendency of people to take more risks once another party has agreed to provide protection. Regulatory interventions to bail out failing firms are often said to create moral hazard, on the assumption that others will expect to be saved from their mistakes, too.

Mortgage-backed security (MBS)—A bond backed by a pool of mortgage loans. The bondholders receive a share of the interest and principal payments on the underlying mortgages. The cash flows may be divided among different classes of bonds, called tranches.

Mutual fund—An investing company that pools the funds of individuals and other investors, and uses them to purchase large amounts of debt or equity obligations of businesses and sometimes debt obligations of governments. The owners of the mutual fund hold proportional shares in the entire pool of securities in which a fund invests. Owners pay taxes on their distributions from a fund; the mutual fund itself is not normally subject to federal or state income taxation.

Naked option—The sale of a call or put option without holding an equal and opposite position in the underlying instrument.

Operational risk—The possibility that a financial institution will suffer losses from a failure to process transactions properly, from accounting mistakes, from rogue traders or other forms of insider fraud, or from other causes arising inside the institution.

Over-the-counter (OTC)—Trading that does not occur on a centralized exchange or trading facility. OTC transactions can occur electronically or over the telephone.

Ponzi Scheme—Named after Charles Ponzi, a man with a remarkable criminal career in the early 20th century, the term has been used to describe pyramid arrangements whereby an enterprise makes payments to investors from the proceeds of a later investment rather than from profits of the underlying business venture, as the investors expected, and gives investors the impression that a legitimate profit-making business or investment opportunity exists, where in fact it is a mere fiction.

Receivership—When an insolvent financial institution is taken over with the intent to liquidate its assets.

Resolution Trust Corporation (RTC) - The agency set up to resolve savings and loans declared failed beginning in 1989. Between 1989 and mid-1995, the Resolution Trust Corporation closed or otherwise resolved 747 thrifts with total assets of $394 billion.

Savings association—A savings and loan association, mutual savings bank, or federal savings bank, whose primary function has traditionally been to encourage personal saving (thrift) and home buying through mortgage lending. In recent years, such institutions' charters have been expanded to allow them to provide commercial loans and a broader range of consumer financial services. The federal regulator for most savings associations is the Office of Thrift Supervision. Also known as savings and loans, thrifts, and mutual savings banks.

Securities Investor Protection Corporation (SIPC)—A private nonprofit membership corporation set up under federal law to provide financial protection for the customers of failed brokers and/or dealers. SIPC is a liquidator; it has no supervisory or regulatory responsibilities for its members, nor is it authorized to bail out or in other ways assist a failing firm.

Securitization—The process of transforming a cash flow, typically from debt repayments, into a new marketable security. Holders of the securitized instrument receive interest and principal payments as the underlying loans are repaid. Types of loans that are frequently securitized are home mortgages, credit card receivables, student loans, small business loans, and car loans.

Self-regulatory organizations (SROs)—National securities or futures exchanges, national securities or futures associations, clearing agencies and the Municipal Securities Rulemaking Board are all authorized to make and enforce rules governing market participants. The respective federal regulatory agency has authority in connection with SROs and may require them to adopt or modify their rules. Examples of SROs in the securities industry include the Financial Industry Regulatory Authority (FINRA), and the New York Stock Exchange.

Special-purpose entities (SPEs)—Also referred to as off–balance-sheet arrangements, SPEs are legal entities created to perform a specific financial function or transaction. They isolate financial risk from the sponsoring institution and provide less-expensive financing. The assets, liabilities, and cash flows of an SPE do not appear on the sponsoring institution's books.

Speculation—a venture or undertaking of an enterprising nature, especially one involving considerable financial risk on the chance of unusual profit.

State regulation—Under the dual system of bank regulation, states as well as the federal government may charter, regulate, and supervise depository institutions. States are the primary regulators in the insurance field. States also have authority over securities companies, mortgage lending companies, personal finance companies, and other types of companies offering financial services.

Structured debt—Debt that has been customized for the buyer, often by incorporating complex derivatives.

Subordinated debt—Debt over which senior debt takes priority. In the event of bankruptcy, subordinated debtholders receive payment only after senior debt claims are paid in full.

Subsidiary—A company whose controlling shares are owned 50% or more by another ("parent") corporation. Like companies with less than 50% ownership, it is an affiliate of the controlling company. A subsidiary is usually consolidated for regulatory and reporting purposes with its parent.

Systemic Risk—The term "systemic risk" does not have a single, agreed-upon definition. Some define systemic risk as the risk an institution faces that it cannot diversify against. In other circumstances, systemic risk is defined as the risk that the linkages between institutions may affect the financial system as a whole, through a dynamic sometimes referred to as contagion.

Thrift holding company—Also known as a savings and loan holding company, a business that controls one or more savings associations. These holding companies are regulated under the Home Owners' Loan Act by the Office of Thrift Supervision.

Too-big-to-fail doctrine—an implicit regulatory policy holding that very large financial institutions must be rescued by the government, because their failure would destabilize the entire financial system. (See "moral hazard.")

Umbrella supervision—The term applied to comprehensive regulation of a holding company and its parts by one or more holding company regulator(s).

Underwriter—For securities markets, see investment bankers. For insurance, underwriters are the life, health and property-casualty companies that receive premiums and pay off losses and other risks as they occur. The underwriters bear the risks of losses and expenses exceeding receipts.

Unitary thrift holding company (UTHC)—A holding company that owns a single thrift institution. A distinction between UTHCs and other thrift holding companies has been that a UTHC could be involved in any lines of business, whereas the others have been restricted to certain activities primarily financial in nature. The Gramm-Leach-Bliley Act limits the commercial activities and affiliations of new UTHCs.

Universal bank—An organizational model typical of some foreign countries whereby a bank can exist as an operating enterprise and own directly a variety of other businesses (See Subsidiary). It contrasts with the banking model typical in the United States where the parent holding company owns several different businesses, all structurally separate (See "affiliate."). In practice, the two approaches are not exclusive.

ACKNOWLEDGMENTS

The authors gratefully acknowledge helpful comments from our colleagues Walter Eubanks, Marc Labonte, and Maureen Murphy.

End Notes

[1] See, e.g., U.S. Treasury, *Blueprint for a Modernized Financial Regulatory Structure*, March 2008, http://www.treas.gov/press/releases/reports/Blueprint.pdf; Group of Thirty, *Financial Reform: A Framework for Financial Stability*, January 2009, http://www.group30.org/pubs/recommendations.pdf; Congressional Oversight Panel, *Special Report on Regulatory Reform*, January 2009, http://cop.senate.gov/documents/cop-012909-report-regulatoryreform.pdf; and Government Accountability Office, *Financial Regulation: A Framework for Crafting and Assessing Proposals to Modernize the Outdated U.S. Financial Regulatory System*, GAO-09-310T, January 14, 2009.

[2] Remarks by Treasury Secretary Timothy Geithner Introducing the Financial Stability Plan, February 10, 2009, http://www.ustreas.gov/press/releases/tg18.htm.

[3] Examples of potential disruptions that markets appear to have handled with relative resilience include the stock market crash of 1987, during which the stock ticker "ran late," and more recent concern that the trading technology for credit default swaps might not be able to process the volume of obligations if a large institution such as Fannie Mae or Freddie Mac suffered a credit event. Currently, the Federal Reserve oversees a domestic interbank clearing system for banks while the CFTC and the SEC oversee trading exchanges for commodities and securities respectively.

[4] Regulatory uses of "capital" include more specific definitions and classifications.

[5] See CRS Report RL33278, *The Basel Accords: The Implementation of II and the Modification of I*, by Walter W. Eubanks.

[6] See CRS Report RL34485, *Basel II in the United States: Progress Toward a Workable Framework*, by Walter W. Eubanks.

[7] National Futures Association, *NFA Manual/Rules*, Section 7001. http://www.nfa.futures.org/nfaManual/ manualFinancial.asp#fins1.

[8] See Sections 1142 and 1143 of the Housing and Economic Recovery Act of 2008, P.L. 110-289.

[9] Section 135 of the Emergency Economic Stabilization Act of 2008 (EESA, P.L. 110-343).

[10] FDICIA created a new section 13(c)(4) of the Federal Deposit Insurance Act,12 USC § 1823(c)(4)(G).

[11] "FDIC Announces Plan to Free Up Bank Liquidity," press release, October 14, 2008, http://www.fdic.gov/news/ news/press/2008/pr08100.html.

[12] The scope of federal preemption has been the subject of recent court decisions. See CRS Report RS22485, *Watters v. Wachovia Bank, N.A.*, by M. Maureen Murphy.

[13] See CRS Report RL34420, *Bear Stearns: Crisis and "Rescue" for a Major Provider of Mortgage-Related Products*, by Gary Shorter.

[14] See CRS Report RL34427, *Financial Turmoil: Federal Reserve Policy Responses*, by Marc Labonte

[15] SEC, "Holding Company Supervision Program Description: Consolidated Supervised Entities ("CSEs")," http://www.sec.gov/divisions/marketreg/hcsupervision.htm.

[16] The Market Reform Act of 1990 permits the SEC to collect certain financial information from unregulated affiliates of broker/dealers, under the Broker-Dealer Risk Assessment Program.

[17] Some argue that CSE allowed the investment banks to hold less capital and increase their leverage. For two views on this issue, see Stephen Labaton, "Agency's '04 Rule Let Banks Pile Up New Debt, and Risk," *New York Times*, October 3, 2008, p. A1, and: Testimony of SEC Chairman Christopher Cox, House Oversight and Government Reform Committee, October 23, 2008. (Response to question from Rep. Christopher Shays.)

[18] By becoming bank holding companies, Morgan Stanley and Goldman Sachs placed themselves under Federal Reserve regulation, presumably to signal to the markets that their financial condition was being monitored.

[19] SEC, "Chairman Cox Announces End of Consolidated Supervised Entities Program," press release 2008-230.

[20] For more on GSEs and their regulation, see CRS Reports CRS Report RS21724, *GSE Regulatory Reform: Frequently Asked Questions*, by N. Eric Weiss, and CRS Report RS21663, *Government-Sponsored Enterprises (GSEs): An Institutional Overview*, by Kevin R. Kosar.

[21] See CRS Report RS22950, *Fannie Mae and Freddie Mac in Conservatorship*, by Mark Jickling.

[22] P.L. 95-630, 92 STAT. 3641.

[23] Executive Order 12631, March 18, 1988, 53 FR 9421.

[24] President's Working Group on Financial Markets, "Policy Statement on Financial Market Developments," March 2008, *http://www.ustreas.gov/press/releases/* reports/pwgpolicystatemktturmoil_03122008.pdf.

[25] Bank for International Settlements, *Triennial Central Bank Survey: Foreign exchange and derivatives market activity,* December 2007, p. 1, http://www.bis.org/publ/rpfxf07t.pdf.

[26] http://www.newyorkfed.org/aboutthefed/fedpoint/fed02.html.

[27] Federal Reserve Bank of New York, "Federal Reserve Announces Establishment of Primary Dealer Credit Facility," Press Release, March 16, 2008. http://www.newyork fed.org/newsevents/news/markets/2008/rp080316.html.

[28] Bank for International Settlements, *Quarterly Review*, December 2008, p. A103. http://www.bis. org/publ/qtrpdf/ r_qt0812.htm.

[29] See CRS Report RS22932, *Credit Default Swaps: Frequently Asked Questions*, by Edward V. Murphy.

[30] CRS Report RL34427, *Financial Turmoil: Federal Reserve Policy Responses*, by Marc Labonte.

[31] Weakening underwriting standards are just one of many explanations for the housing bubble, including unsustainable capital flows that may have been due to a global savings glut or monetary policies that may have been too expansionary for too long.

[32] See CRS Report RS22722, *Securitization and Federal Regulation of Mortgages for Safety and Soundness*, by Edward V. Murphy.

[33] See CRS Report 94-511, *Hedge Funds: Should They Be Regulated?*, by Mark Jickling.

[34] United States Senate, Permanent Subcommittee on Investigations of the Committee on Homeland Security and Governmental Affairs, *Staff Report: Excessive Speculation in the Natural Gas Market*, June 25, 2007.

[35] The Comptrollers handbooks are occasionally updated. The most recent handbook for the Bank Supervision Process is dated September 2007 and can be found at *http://www.occ.gov/* handbook/banksup.pdf.

In: International Perspectives on Financial... ISBN: 978-1-61728-006-1
Editor: James P. Corrigan © 2011 Nova Science Publishers, Inc.

Chapter 2

FINANCIAL MARKET SUPERVISION: EUROPEAN PERSPECTIVES*

James K. Jackson

SUMMARY

The global financial crisis has sparked a debate over the cause and impact of the crisis. Academics and policymakers are searching for changes in the financial system that can correct any perceived weaknesses in the structure of regulation, the content of regulations, and the coverage of financial instruments and activities. Since the onset of the crisis, numerous proposals have been advanced to reform or amend the current financial system to help restore economic growth. In the United States, the Obama Administration has proposed a plan to overhaul supervision of the U.S. financial services sector. The proposal would give new authority to the Federal Reserve, create a new Financial Services Oversight Council, create a Consumer Financial Protection Agency, and create a new National Bank Supervisor to replace the Office of the Comptroller of the Currency and the Office of Thrift Supervision. In contrast, Senator Collins introduced S. 664, the Financial System Stabilization and Reform Act of 2009, with a companion measure, H.R. 1754, that was introduced by Representative Castle in the House of Representatives. The

---

* This is an edited, reformatted and augmented version of a CRS Report for Congress publication dated November 2009.

measures would create a Financial Stability Council and grant the Federal Reserve the authority to examine the soundness and safety of the financial system posed by bank holding companies. Other measures include: S. 1682 (Senator Cantwell), the Derivatives Market Manipulation Prevention Act of 2009; S. 1803 (Senator Merkley), the Federal Reserve Accountability Act of 2009; S. 2756 (Senator Warner) the Financial Services Systemic Risk Oversight Council Act of 2009; H.R. 3795 (Representative Frank), the Over-the-Counter Derivatives Markets Acts of 2009; H.R. 3968 (Representative Ellison), to amend the Bank Holding Company Act; and H.R. 3996 (Frank), to improve financial stability. The crisis has underscored the fact that national and international financial markets have become highly integrated, and problems in one market can trigger contagion that can spread both among countries and into economic sectors to affect businesses, employment, and household well being.

Similarly, governments in Europe are considering what, if any, changes they should make to their national financial systems. Along with the United States and other countries, European countries also are considering changes to the international systems of financial supervision and regulation in order to ensure prosperity through the smooth operation of domestic and international financial systems. This process may include reconsidering the roles and responsibility of the central banks in the post-financial crisis era. Various organizations and groups are advancing a large number of recommendations and prescriptions. Some goals for any such adjustments may include providing an institutional structure for oversight and regulation that is robust, comprehensive, flexible, and politically feasible while providing appropriate incentive structures to preclude excessive risk- taking. Of course, there are no guarantees that amending the current system or employing a different regulatory and supervisory structure will preclude a repeat of the most recent financial crisis given that financial markets and institutions are continually growing, innovating, and responding to government- and market-imposed constraints.

This report addresses the European perspectives on a number of proposals that are being advanced for financial oversight and regulation in Europe. The European experience may be instructive because financial markets in Europe are well developed, European firms often are competitors of U.S. firms, and European governments have faced severe problems of integration and consistency across the various financial structures that exist in Europe.

OVERVIEW

The global financial crisis has resulted in huge losses in wealth, jobs, and economic activity. In some cases, it has led to public demonstrations and to changes in national governments. Academics and policymakers generally agree that the financial system can benefit from additional supervision or regulation that addresses issues of systemic risk. Such efforts, however, likely will require hard, and possibly politically unpopular, decisions concerning the supervision and regulation of domestic financial markets and new layers of international coordination that could challenge entrenched national interests. Furthermore, there are no metrics for gauging whether such measures are a prescription for curing the current crisis or are a policy framework for preventing the next crisis, since financial markets are constantly innovating and responding to regulation and oversight. In addition, there are no models of market oversight or supervision that have proven to be clearly superior. In the absence of such a model, policymakers face a blizzard of recommendations, but few assurances that changes to domestic and international financial frameworks, most likely achieved with considerable institutional and political resistance, will preclude another crisis.

Currently, national governments are using a number of approaches to supervise financial markets. While the current situation is quite fluid, there seems to be some movement in national supervisory frameworks toward an integrated approach, as used in Great Britain and Germany. Regardless of which structural form is employed, regulating financial activities at the national level is complicated by the nature of modern financial markets that have become highly complex and interdependent. While regulation is set largely in a national context, financial institutions are international in their activities. Without consistent regulatory standards across national boundaries, banks, insurers, and securities companies can move their activities to jurisdictions with looser standards. National governments, however, generally are loathe to cede sovereignty to any supra-national institution, and efforts to reshape national financial authorities often face stiff opposition from entrenched interest groups.

Furthermore, national financial markets are not clones of one another, but reflect differences in the way they have been organized and philosophical differences over the way they are regulated and supervised. Indeed, national financial markets are custom-made structures that reflect differences in national experiences, government institutions, laws, and national customs. One thing the crisis has demonstrated, though, is that despite these differences, financial markets have become highly integrated. As a result, it has become increasingly more difficult, as evidenced by the current financial crisis, to contain financial problems in one market from affecting markets in seemingly unrelated areas.

The European Union has taken a number of steps to improve financial supervision among its members, including: strengthening the roles of advisory Committees in the areas of securities, banking, and insurance regulators; adopting regulations on credit rating agencies; providing funding in support of international accounting standards; and considering a measure to register hedge funds. The EU also adopted a proposal to have a European Systemic Risk Council and a European System of Financial Supervisors that will serve as advisors to EC members in providing advice in both macro and micro prudential supervision. The United States has chosen to take a different approach that could potentially strengthen the role of the Federal Reserve and create a new consumer watchdog agency, among other proposals.

THE EUROPEAN UNION

The European Union (EU) is a political and economic union of 27 member states, formally established in 1993 by the Treaty of Maastricht out of existing structures that had evolved in steps since the 1950s. The EU has worked to develop a single economic market through a standardized system of laws which apply across all member states and which provide the freedom of movement of people, goods, services and capital. This process of economic integration is complicated by a dual system that gives the members of the EU significant independence within the EU and broad discretion to interpret and implement EU directives. EU economic integration is compounded further by sixteen member states, collectively known as the Eurozone[1], which have adopted the euro as a common currency and operate as a bloc within the EU. Major institutions and bodies of the EU include the European Commission, the European Parliament, the Council of the European Union, the European Council, the European Court of Justice, and the European Central Bank (ECB). Through various Directives, the EU has moved to increase financial integration within the Union to make the monetary union represented by the Eurozone operate more efficiently.

Within the EU, the European Commission operates as the executive branch and is responsible for proposing legislation, implementing decisions, upholding the Union's treaties, and the general day-to-day running of the Union. The Commission operates as a cabinet government, with one Commissioner from each member. One of the 27 is the Commission President (currently José Manuel Barroso) appointed by the European Council, with the approval of the European Parliament, for a term of five years. Relative to the financial sector, the EU process provides for each member to have its own institutional and legal framework, which complicates efforts to coordinate financial policies. The Economic and Financial Affairs Council (ECOFIN) is one of the oldest bodies within the European Council. ECOFIN is responsible for economic policy coordination, economic surveillance, monitoring budget policy and preparing the EU's budget.

There are three main procedures the EU uses to enact legislation. These procedures are codecision, assent, and consultation. The co-decision procedure, also known as the Article 251 procedure (Article 251 of the Treaty of Rome), is the main legislative process the EU employs to adopt directives and regulations. The Council and the European Parliament jointly adopt legislation based on a proposal by the European Commission. Both Parliament and the Council are required to agree on an identical bill before the measure can be adopted. In general terms, Parliament is considered to have adopted a measure if it fails to reject the proposed measure within three months after it has been adopted by the Council. Under the assent procedure, the Council can adopt a measure proposed by the Commission if it receives the assent of Parliament. Under the consultation procedure, the Council, acting unanimously or as a qualified majority, can adopt legislation developed by the Commission after it has consulted with Parliament.

Since the start of the financial crisis, the European Union has taken a number of steps to improve supervision of financial markets. These actions include:

- Strengthened the Committee of European Securities Regulators. The Committee is an advisory body without any regulatory authority within the European Commission. The Directive of January 23, 2009, strengthened the Committee's authority to mediate and coordinate securities regulations between EU members.
- Strengthened the Committee of European Banking Supervisors. The Committee is an advisory body without any regulatory authority that coordinates banking supervision. The EU Directive of January 23, 2009, broadened the role of the Committee to include supervision of financial conglomerates.

- Strengthened the Committee of European Insurance and Occupational Pensions Supervisors. The Committee is an advisory body without any regulatory authority within the European Commission in the areas of insurance, reinsurance, and occupational pensions fields. The January 23, 2009, Directive authorizes the Committee to coordinate policies among EU members and between the EU and national governments and other bodies.
- The European Parliament and the European Council approved on April 23, 2009 new regulations on credit rating agencies that are expected to improve the quality and transparency of the ratings agencies.
- Approved direct funding by the European Union to the International Accounting Standards Committee Foundation, the European Financial Reporting Advisory Group, and the Public Interest Oversight Body.
- The European Commission proposed a set of measures to register hedge fund managers and managers of alternative investment funds and measures to regulate executive compensation.
- Adopted measures to create a new European Systemic Risk Board (ESRB) and a European System of Financial Supervisors. The European Central Bank has been entrusted with providing analytical, statistical, administrative, and logistical support to the ESRB.

The euro area countries initially sketched out a broad response to the financial crisis. Since then, their response to bank foreclosures and to subsequent issues has been characterized by some as somewhat disjointed. The financial crisis and economic downturn have exposed deep fissures within the EU and even within the euro area countries over the policy course to follow. As a first response to the financial crisis, EU governments and their central banks focused policy initiatives on reassuring credit markets that there was an availability of credit and liquidity, by reducing interest rates, and by providing foreign currency, primarily dollars, through currency arrangements. In addition to continuing efforts to restore the financial markets, EU members also face a worsening economic climate that has required actions by individual central banks, international organizations, and coordinated actions by EU members and other governments.

FINANCIAL CRISIS

As the loss of real and financial wealth worsened, EU governments worked both independently and in tandem to protect financial institutions and to sustain economic growth. The actions EU leaders take are important to the United States, because EU members comprise some of the largest financial centers in the world, their financial markets are well developed, and European financial firms are often competitors to those in the United States. The economic and financial crises, however, have exposed deep philosophical differences among EU members over the most effective policy course to pursue to address the financial crisis and the economic downturn and problems of integration and consistency across countries. In part, these differences reflect the dual nature of the EU system, which gives great deference to the individual members of the EU in interpreting and implementing EU Directives. Unlike the United States, where the Federal government can implement policies that are applied systematically across all 50 States, EU-wide actions reflect compromise among 27 national authorities.[2]

The financial crisis has made EU members especially concerned about the size and structure of financial systems and they are pursuing changes to the international financial system. Financial systems have become large, complex, interconnected structures that have grown so large that some observers question whether the current financial system is compatible with maintaining financial stability. They also raise concerns about the ability of national governments to restrain the impact of financial firms on public resources should major financial firms face periods of serious distress. The United Kingdom and the United States, for instance, are the two largest international banking centers in the world. As such, they operate as major conduits, or as intermediaries, through which capital flows from countries with excess capital to those countries in need of capital. Banking centers in the United Kingdom, Switzerland, and elsewhere are notable because they are large compared to their respective national gross domestic product (GDP) and large compared to the relative size of banking centers in the United States. Bank assets in Switzerland, for instance, are nearly nine times the size of the country's GDP, while such assets are over four times GDP in the United Kingdom. In Spain, Germany, France, and Ireland, bank assets are at least double GDP, while such assets run less than 60% of GDP in the United States. In an effort to address the prospect that large banks or financial firms may become insolvent or fail and, thereby, cause a major disruption to the financial system, the British Parliament in February 2009 passed the Banking Act of 2009. The act makes permanent a set of procedures the U.K. Government had developed to deal with troubled banks before they become insolvent or collapse. Such procedures are being considered by other EU governments and others as they amend their respective supervisory frameworks.

Within the EU system, the greatest share of responsibility for regulating and supervising financial markets rest with the national governments. National authorities implement EU Directives in ways they determine are consistent with their own national objectives and national interests, not necessarily to benefit the EU as a whole. As a consequence of this focus at the national level, there is some potential for nations to act in their own interests at the expense of other EU members, especially during periods of financial and economic distress. The financial crisis also has aggravated conflicts between broad EU-wide goals and the more focused national objectives of the individual EU members. For instance, as financial markets faced serious shortages of liquidity, EU members were pressed to support a broad set of measures to increase the guarantees on bank accounts for depositors in response to actions by Ireland, Greece, and Germany. In addition, some EU members have been considering a set of procedures to deal with the bad loans of banks within their jurisdictions, which has pushed the EU as a whole to follow suit and consider the best approach to deal with the toxic loans of EU banks. These differences may well become more pronounced as multilateral discussions shift from addressing the general goal of containing the financial crisis to the more contentious issues of specific market reforms, regulations, and supervision.

The globalization of financial markets raises the stakes for a coordinated response within the EU and between the EU and the United States. In various ways, globalized financial markets challenge the effectiveness of the current framework of financial market supervision and coordination that is based on national interests. Significant differences remain among EU members and between EU members and the United States over the best approach to follow to supervise financial markets. Some EU members favor a strong central authority that can monitor financial markets, while others favor strong national authorities with a weaker role for an international body.

The EU approach is also complicated by the requirement that new policies must mesh with the carefully crafted and highly negotiated Directives that already exist within the EU framework. These Directives act as guiding principles for EU members, and include the Stability and Growth Pact[3], the Lisbon Principles,[4] and the Financial Services Action Plan.[5] Arguably, these agreements have helped stabilize economic conditions in Europe by bringing down the overall rate of price inflation and by reducing government budget deficits. In addition to these Directives, the EU members have adopted a series of measures that deal directly with an EU-wide effort to coordinate financial policies across all the EU members.

As part of the overall EU effort to achieve financial and economic integration, the EU members have adopted such Directives as the Directive on Financial Services and the Financial Services Action Plan (FSAP).The integration of the financial services sector across borders, however, has been uneven, with integration progressing faster in the money, bond, and equity markets, and slower in the banking sector where much of the focus on international cooperation is being directed. According to the European Central Bank,[6] retail banking services remain segmented along national lines as a result of differences in national tax laws, costs of national registration and compliance, and cultural preferences. Nevertheless, cross-border mergers and acquisitions within Europe have played an important role in internationalizing banking groups, which has led to significant cross-border banking activity. Integration within the banking sector in Europe also has increased since the euro-area countries adopted the euro as their single currency.

Other Major EU Financial Directives

Investment Services Directive

The EU has adopted a number of directives that provide a basic framework for EU members to coordinate financial regulation across the EU and to integrate financial sectors. One such directive is the Investment Services Directive (ISD) that entered into force on January 1, 1996. The ISD provided general principles for national securities regulations, with the goal of providing mutual recognition of regulations across the EU.[7] The ISD created a "European Passport" that provided for a cross-border right of establishment for non-bank investment firms and the freedom to provide services across borders for investment firms to carry out a wide range of investment business. Under the passport, firms were authorized and supervised by domestic authorities, but could still provide specified investment services in other EU countries. Such cross border services included: collecting and executing buy and sell orders on an agency basis; dealing, managing and underwriting portfolios; and such additional services as providing investment advice, advising on mergers and acquisitions, safekeeping and administration of securities, and foreign exchange transactions.

The European "passport" provision required member states to dismantle restrictive legislation that prevented cross-border branching and freedom of services. Nevertheless, EU members retained the responsibility for determining their own domestic laws and regulations concerning such issues as fitness, authorization, capital requirements, and protection of client assets. EU members could also impose rules and regulations on investment firms using the European passport as long as the rules and regulations were, "in the interest of the general good," and applied to the business activities that the firms carried out in their state. The ISD opened up stock exchange membership in all member states to all types of investment firms, whether bank or non- bank entities. Another objective of the ISD was to eliminate the so-called concentration rule in order to allow member states that lacked their own securities trading floor to access electronic terminals with investment firms and banks in other member states, thereby allowing them to be members of the markets on a remote electronic basis.

Financial Services Action Plan

In 1999, the EU replaced the Investment Services Directive with the Financial Services Action Plan (FSAP). The Plan consists of a set of measures that are intended to remove the remaining formal barriers in financial markets among EU members and to provide a legal and regulatory environment that supports the integration of EU financial markets.[8] Similar to the ISD, the FSAP process supports a two pronged approach that combines EU directives with national laws. The EU directives provide for a general level of regulation concerning the provision of financial services across borders and the harmonization of national regulations governing cross-border activities. EU members, however, retain the right to regulate firms within their own borders, as long as those firms, whether foreign or domestic, are treated equally. The FSAP contains 42 articles, 38 of which were implemented, that are intended to meet 3 specific objectives: (1) a single wholesale market; (2) an open and secure retail market; and (3) state-of-the art rules and supervision. Wholesale measures relate to securities issuance and trading; securities settlement; accounts; and corporate restructuring. Retail measures relate to insurance; savings through pension funds and mutual funds; retail payments; electronic money; and money laundering.

Markets in Financial Instruments Directive

The cornerstone of the FSAP 's achievement is the Markets in Financial Instruments Directive (MiFID), which became effective on November 1, 2007.

The MiFID establishes a comprehensive, harmonized set of rules for Europe's securities markets so financial services firms can provide investment services in each of the EU member states. MiFID retained the principles of the EU "passport" and extended the list of services and financial instruments that are covered by the passport procedures, including investment advice. MiFID also removed the so- called concentration rule that required investment firms to route all stock transactions through established exchanges.

MiFID introduced the concept of 'maximum harmonization' which places more emphasis on home state supervision. This is a change from the prior EU financial service legislation which featured a "minimum harmonization and mutual recognition" concept. Minimum harmonization provides for a law or a regulation that sets a floor, or a minimum standard, that EU countries were expected to meet in developing legislation. Maximum harmonization provides for a maximum level of a law or a regulation that sets the maximum allowable standard that can be adopted in domestic laws or regulations. At times some EU members have been accused of adopting domestic measures that exceed the EU standard in a manner that acted as a protectionist barrier.

Some key elements of the MiFID are:

- Authorization, regulation and passporting. Firms covered by MiFID are authorized and regulated in their "home state." Once a firm is authorized, it can use the MiFID passport to provide services to customers in other EU member states. These services are regulated by the "home state" in which the firm is authorized.
- Client categorization. MiFID requires firms to categorize clients as "eligible counter-parties," professional clients, or retail clients, with increasing levels of protection.
- Client order handling. MiFID places requirements on information that needs to be captured when firms accept client orders in order to ensure that a firm is acting in a client's best interests.
- Pre-trade transparency. MiFID requires the operators of various kinds of equity exchanges to make the best bid and offer prices available to potential buyers and sellers.
- Post-trade transparency. MiFID requires firms to publish the price, volume and time of all trades in listed shares, even if executed outside of a regulated market, unless certain requirements are met to allow for deferred publication.
- Best execution. MiFID will require that firms take all reasonable steps to obtain the best possible result in the execution of an order for a

client. The best possible result is not limited to execution price but also includes cost, speed, likelihood of execution and likelihood of settlement and any other factors deemed relevant.

- Systematic Internalizer. A Systematic Internalizer is a firm that executes orders from its clients against its own book or against orders from other clients and are treated as mini-exchanges, which makes them subject to pre-trade and post-trade transparency requirements

Capital Requirements Directive

The Capital Requirements Directive, which became effective in January 2007, introduced a supervisory framework within the EU for investment management firms and banks. The purpose of the Directive is to move the EU towards complying with the Basel II[9] rules on capital measurement, adequacy, and related market disclosure disciplines. This Directive promotes a risk based capital management methodology through a "three pillar" structure that includes (1) new standards that set out the minimum capital requirements that firms will be required to meet for credit, market, and operational risk; (2) requirements that firms and supervisors must decide whether they are holding enough capital to address the risks realized under Pillar I and act accordingly; and (3) requirements that firms publish certain details about their risks, capital, and risk management. The Directive also requires firms to make provision for a charge against their capital for operational risks in order to identify, monitor, manage, and report on certain types of external events that may have a negative effect on their capital. The Directive applies not only to internationally active banks, which is the main focus of the Basel II approach, but it also applies to all credit institutions and investment firms irrespective of the size, scope of activities, or levels of sophistication. Under the Directive, firms are required to meet rules governing the minimum amounts of their own financial resources they must have in order to cover the risks to which they may be exposed.

EU Financial Supervisory Authorities

Within the EU, there are a number of bodies that bring together the supervisors, finance ministers, and central bankers of the EU members, as indicated in Figure 1. These bodies are under the direction of the European Commission and the Ministries of Finance of the individual EU members, while they also are subject to the central banks and National Supervisors[10] of each EU member. Within the European Council, the Economic and Financial Affairs Council (ECOFIN) is one of the oldest bodies associated with the Council. ECOFIN is responsible for coordinating economic policy, performing economic surveillance, and for monitoring budget policy and preparing the EU's budget. The key bodies in the EU banking sector include the following:

- **European Banking Committee.** The committee consists of representatives of the ministries of finance of the EU members and advises the EU Commission on policy issues related to banking activities and on proposals in the banking area.

- **Committee of European Banking Supervision**. The committee is comprised of representatives of supervisory authorities and central banks and coordinates on regulatory and supervisory convergence.

- **European Central Bank.** The ECB's main role is financial stability and monitoring in cooperation with national central banks and supervisory agencies.

- **Banking Supervision Committee.** This committee brings together national central banks, banking supervisory authorities, and the ECB. It monitors and assesses developments in the euro area, analyses the impact of regulatory and supervisory requirements on financial system stability, and it promotes cooperation and exchange of information between central banks and supervisory authorities on issues of common interest.

- **Economic and Financial Committee.** The committee includes representatives of ministries of finance, the European Commission, the ECB, and central banks to promote high-level assessments of developments in financial markets.

- **Financial Stability Table.** This body meets twice a year to discuss financial stability issues.

- **Financial Services Committee.** This committee is composed of representatives of the ministries of finance and the European Commission and discusses and provides guidance on cross-sector strategic and policy issues.

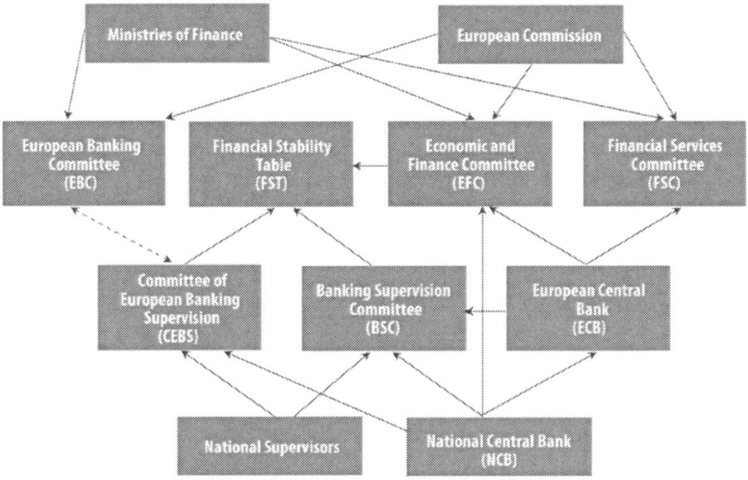

Source: OECD Economic Studies: Euro Area, Organization for Economic Cooperation and Development, 2009.

Figure 1. Key Bodies in the EU Banking Sector-Stability Framework

In addition to the committees and bodies indicated in Figure 1, there are other components to the EU financial structure. Some EU members have negotiated Memorandum of Understanding (MOU) agreements that commit the parties to a regular exchange of information and to consultation on enforcement of regulations. EU members also have developed "Colleges" of supervisors that represent each EU member in coordinating policies on financial activities that cross national borders, principally in such specific areas of financial services as insurance and banking. In addition, three financial services committees organized under the so-called Lamfalussy process[11] promote financial sector integration in the banking, insurance, and securities sectors. These committees are designated as Level 3 committees since they operate at the third stage in a process designed to coordinate efforts among the EU members in order to build support to implement legislation.

Within the EU, the structure of financial market supervision varies markedly, as indicated in Table 1. Likewise, the objectives and mandates of the supervisory authorities, the central banks, the Ministries of Finance, and other organizations also vary by individual country, according to a staff report prepared by the International Monetary Fund. [12] Among the 27 members of the EU, a little more than half have a single supervisory authority overseeing the banking sector, while slightly less than half have a sectoral model, or a supervisory authority that focuses on a particular segment of the financial services industry. The central bank is involved in supervising the financial markets in every EU country, but it acts as a supervisory authority in only half of the members. In all of the EU members, the banking supervisory authority supervises banks and insurance providers and in all but one country, the supervisory authority also supervises securities firms. In slightly fewer countries, the banking supervisory authority also supervises the management of pension funds. Also, in nearly every EU country, the banking supervisory authority is responsible for maintaining stability in the financial system and for protecting the deposits and other interests of consumers. Fewer than half of the banking supervisory authorities are responsible for supervising the conduct of firms within the financial sector and only about one-third are responsible for maintaining or ensuring that there is competition in the market.

The "European Framework for Action"

As an initial response to the financial crisis, the European Commission released on October 29, 2008, its "European Framework for Action" as a way to coordinate the actions of the 27 member states of the European Union.[13] On November 16, 2008, the Commission announced a more detailed plan that brings together short-term goals to address the current economic downturn with the longer-term goals on growth and jobs that are integral to the Lisbon Strategy for Growth and Jobs that was adopted by the EU in 2000 and recast in 2005.[14] The short-term plan focuses on a three-part approach to an overall EU recovery action plan/framework. The three parts to the EU framework are:

- **A new financial market architecture at the EU level**. The basis of this architecture involves implementing measures that EU members have announced as well as providing for: (1) continued support for the financial system from the European Central Bank and other central banks; (2) rapid and consistent implementation of the bank rescue plan that has been established by the member states; and (3) decisive measures that are designed to contain the crisis from spreading to all of the member states. As the financial system is stabilized, the next step is to restructure the banking sector and to return banks to the private sector. Proposals include: deposit guarantees and capital requirements; regulation and accounting standards; credit rating agencies; executive pay; capital market supervision; and risk management.

Table 1. European Union Financial Supervisory Structures

Country	Supervisory structure			Central bank as supervisory authority	Central bank involvement	Main tasks/areas of supervision of banking supervisory authority							
	Sectoral odel	Model by objectives	Single Authority			Banking supervision	Pension fund supervision	Insurance supervision	Securities supervision	Stability	Conduct of business	Consumer protection	Market competition
Austria			×	×	×	×	×	×	×	×	×	×	
Belgium			×		×	×	×	×	×		×	×	×
Bulgaria	×			×	×	×	×	×	×	×		×	
Czech Rep.			×	×	×	×	×	×	×	×	×		×
Cyprus	×			×	×	×	×	×	×	×		×	×
Denmark			×		×	×	×	×	×	×	×	×	
Estonia			×		×	×		×	×	×	×	×	
Finland	×				×	×		×	×	×	×	×	
France	×				×	×		×	×	×		×	
Germany			×	×	×	×		×	×	×	×	×	
Greece	×			×	×	×		×	×	×	×	×	
Hungary			×		×	×	×	×	×	×	×	×	×
Ireland			×		×	×		×	×	×		×	×
Italy	×			×	×	×	×	×	×	×	×	×	×

Table 1. (Continued)

Country	Supervisory structure			Central bank as supervisory authority	Central bank involvement	Main tasks/areas of supervision of banking supervisory authority							
	Sectoral model	Model by objectives	Single Authority			Banking supervision	Pension fund supervision	Insurance supervision	Securities supervision	Stability	Conduct of business	Consumer protection	Market competition
Lithuania	×			×	×	×		×	×	×		×	×
Latvia			×		×	×	×	×	×	×		×	
Luxembourg						×	×	×	×	×		×	
Malta			×		×	×		×	×		×	×	×
Netherlands		×		×	×	×	×	×	×	×	×	×	×
Poland			×		×	×	×	×	×	×			
Portugal	×	×		×	×	×	×	×	×	×		×	
Romania	×			×	×	×	×	×	×	×			
Slovakia		×	×	×	×	×	×	×	×	×	×	×	
Slovenia	×		×	×	×	×	×	×	×		×		
Spain	×		×	×	×	×	×	×	×		×		
Sweden		×		×	×	×	×	×	×		×		
United Kingdom		×		×	×		×		×		×		

Source: Hardy, Daniel, A "European Mandate" for Financial Sector Authorities in the EU, in *Euro Area Policies: Selected Issues*, International Monetary Fund. IMF Country Report No. 08263, August 2008, p. 76.

- **Dealing with the impact on the real economy.** The policy instruments that can be employed to address the expected rise in unemployment and decline in economic growth are in the hands of the member states. Nevertheless, the EU can assist by adding short-term actions to its structural reform agenda, while investing in the future through: (1) increasing investment in R&D innovation and education; (2) promoting flexicurity[15] to protect and equip people rather than specific jobs; (3) freeing up businesses to build markets at home and internationally; and (4) enhancing competitiveness by promoting green technology, and overcoming energy security constraints and achieving environmental goals. In addition, the Commission will explore a wide range of ways in which EU members can increase their rate of economic growth.
- The impact of the financial crisis on the real economies of the EU members likely will require adjustments to the fiscal and monetary policies of the EU members. The Stability and Growth Pact[16] of the EU members should serve as the blueprint for members facing higher than expected levels of fiscal or monetary stimulus so that such policies should be accompanied by structural reforms. Such reforms should aim to sustain domestic demand in the short-run, ease transitions within and into the labor market, and increase potential growth by directing investment into areas that will sustain employment and advance productivity. Reforms in the finance sector should focus on enhancing the competitive position of the European industry and finance the needs of small and medium-sized firms. The Commission will also attempt to counter an expected increase in unemployment by using funds provided under the European Social Fund[17] to reintroduce unemployed workers back into the work force.

- **A global response to the financial crisis.** The financial crisis has demonstrated the growing interaction between the financial sector and the goods- and services- producing sectors of economies. As a result, the crisis has raised questions concerning global governance that are relative to the financial sector and to the need to maintain open trade markets. The EU used the November 15, 2008 multi- nation economic summit in Washington D.C. to promote a series of measures to reform the global financial architecture. The Commission argued that the measures should include: (1) strengthening international regulatory standards; (2) strengthening international coordination among financial supervisors; (3) strengthening measures to monitor and coordinate macroeconomic policies; and (4) developing the capacity to address financial crises at the national regional and multilateral levels. Also, a financial architecture should be constructed upon three key principles: (1) efficiency; (2) transparency and accountability; and (3) representation in any group should include key emerging economies.

The de Larosiere Report and the European Plan for Recovery

When the European Union released its "Framework for Action" in response to the immediate needs of the financial crisis, it was moving to address the long-term requirements of the financial system. As a key component of this approach, the EU commissioned a group within the EU to assess the weaknesses of the existing EU financial architecture. It also charged this group with developing proposals that could guide the EU in fashioning a system that would provide early warning of areas of financial weakness and chart a way forward in erecting a stronger financial system. As part of this way forward, the European Union issued two reports in the first quarter of 2009 that address the issue of supervision of financial markets. The first report,[18] issued on February 25, 2009, and commissioned by the European Union, was prepared by a High-Level Group on financial supervision headed by former IMF Managing Director and ex-Bank of France Governor Jacques de Larosiere and, therefore, is known as the de Larosiere Report. The second report[19] was published by the European Commission to chart the course ahead for the members of the EU to reform the international financial governance system.

The de Larosiere Report

The de Larosiere Report focused on four main issues: (1) causes of the financial crisis; (2) organizing the supervision of financial institutions and markets in the EU; (3) strengthening European cooperation on financial stability, oversight, early warning, and crisis mechanisms; and (4) organizing EU supervisors to cooperate globally. The report proposed 31 recommendations on regulation and supervision of financial markets. The recommendations are summarized in Appendix.

The report argued that the financial crisis was characterized by a systemic failure to correctly price the risk of financial instruments as a result of plentiful liquidity, low returns, and investors seeking higher yields. Together, these events led to a fundamental failure by financial firms to adequately assess the risks associated with their activities and it exposed a systemic failure on the part of regulators and financial supervisors. In this environment, long-standing practices that relied on the risk management capabilities of the financial institutions themselves and on the adequacy of credit ratings all proved to be inadequate. Too much attention was paid to each individual firm and too little attention was given to the impact of general developments on sectors or markets as a whole. According to the report, "These developments point to serious limitations in the existing supervisory framework globally, both in a national and cross-border context."[20] According to the report:

> Regulators and supervisors focused on the micro-prudential supervision of individual financial institutions and not sufficiently on the macro-systemic risks of a contagion of correlated horizontal shocks. Strong international competition among financial centers also contributed to national regulators and supervisors being reluctant to take unilateral action.[21]

As the financial crisis unfolded, the de Larosiere Report concluded, the regulatory response by the European Union and its members was weakened by, "an inadequate crisis management infrastructure in the EU." Furthermore, the report emphasized that an inconsistent set of rules across the EU as a result of the closely guarded sovereignty of national financial regulators led to a wide diversity of national regulations reflecting local traditions, legislation, and practices. While micro-prudential supervision focused on limiting the distress of individual financial institutions in order to protect the depositors, it neglected the broader objective of macro- prudential supervision, which is aimed at limiting distress to the financial system as a whole in order to protect the economy from significant losses in real output. In order to remedy this obstacle, the report offered a two-level approach to reforming financial market supervision in the EU. This approach centers around new oversight of broad, system-wide risks and a higher-level of coordination among national supervisors involved in day-to-day oversight.

The de Larosiere Report recommended that the EU create a new macro-prudential level of supervision called the European Systemic Risk Council (ESRC) chaired by the President of the European Central Bank, as indicated in Figure 2. This proposal was adopted by the European Commission with some changes, including changing the name to the European Systemic Risk Board (ESRB). A driving force behind creating the ESRB was that it would bring together the central banks of all of the EU members with a clear mandate to preserve financial stability by collectively forming judgments and making recommendations on macro-prudential policy. The ESRB will also gather information on all macro-prudential risks in the EU, decide on macro-prudential policy, provide early risk warning to EU supervisors, compare observations on macroeconomic and prudential developments, and give direction on the aforementioned issues.

The EC also followed the report's recommendation to create a new European System of Financial Supervision (ESFS) to transform a group of EU committees known as L3 Committees[22] into EU Authorities. The three L3 Committees are the Committee of European Securities Regulators (CESR); the Committee of European Banking Supervisors (CEBS); and the Committee of European Insurance and Occupational Pensions Supervisors (CEIOPS). The ESFS will maintain the decentralized structure that characterizes the current system of national supervisors, while the ESFS will coordinate the actions of the national authorities to maintain common high level supervisory standards, guarantee strong cooperation with other supervisors, and guarantee that the interests of the host supervisors are safeguarded.

Under this system, the European Central Bank (ECB) will have no micro-prudential role in supervising banks, but it will lead efforts within the European System of Central Banks (ESCB)[23] on macro-prudential supervision. In part, these macro-prudential activities include: (1) analyzing financial stability; (2) developing an early warning system to signal the emergence of risks and vulnerabilities of the financial sector to specific shocks and to issues that have cross-border and cross-sector dimensions; and (3) developing macro-prudential requirements.

The main tasks of the ESFS authorities are to provide legally binding mediation between national supervisors; adopt binding supervisory standards; adopt binding technical decisions that apply to individual institutions; provide oversight and coordination of colleges of supervisors; license and supervise specific EU-wide institutions; provide binding cooperation with the ESRB to ensure that there is adequate macro-prudential supervision; and assume a strong coordinating role in crisis situations. The main mission of the national supervisors would be to oversee the day-to-day operation of firms.

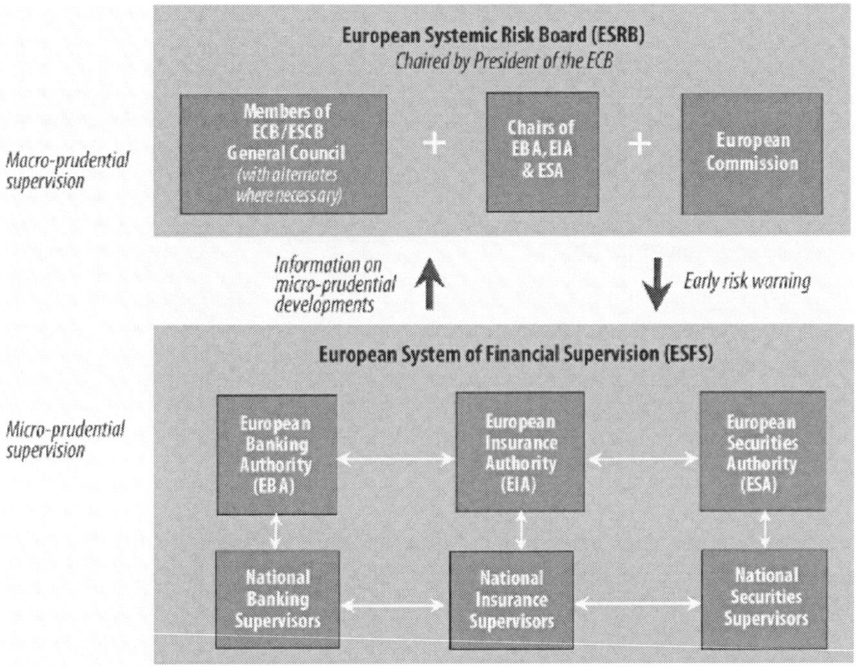

Source: Report, The High-Level Group on Financial Supervision in the EU, February 25, 2009.

Figure 2. European Financial Supervision in the de Larosiere Report

The report envisioned the creation of the ESFS as a multi-year process that would be accomplished in two stages, but this multi-year phase-in was adjusted by the EC to one year in the final legislation. The first stage would have taken a year and would have served to prepare the groundwork for the transformation of the EU supervisory system by strengthening the national supervisors, harmonizing national legislation, strengthening the Level 3 committees, and expanding the use of supervisory colleges. In the second stage, which was expected to take two years to accomplish, the level 3 committees were to be transformed into the three Authorities previously mentioned. In addition to continuing to perform the functions currently assigned to these committees,[24] the new European Authorities would (1) have the authority to resolve disputes between national supervisors regarding financial institutions operating across national borders; (2) be responsible for the licensing and direct supervision of some specific EU-wide institutions; (3) play a decisive role in the interpretation and development of technical standards; (4) be responsible for establishing supervisory standards and practices; (5) work closely with the ESRC to assure that the ESRC can carry out its responsibilities for macro-prudential supervision; (6) facilitate exchanges of information in crisis situations and act as a mediator when necessary; and (7) represent EU interests in bilateral and multilateral discussions relating to financial supervision.

The de Larosiere Report also considered a framework for dealing with distressed or failing banks, especially when those banks have a presence across several national jurisdictions. Typically, the report argued, distressed or failing banks should be handled by national central banks, where they exist, because central banks likely would be the first to see signs of trouble. However, inconsistent crisis management and resolution tools across the EU compound efforts to contain bank crises. Similarly, EU governments have adopted different deposit guarantee schemes that are inconsistent across the EU and seem to be geared toward a minimum coverage level. This inconsistent approach worsens the shift of deposits among banks during periods of perceived weakness and raises the prospect that banks of different national origin that operate within a single country could offer different levels of depositor protection within the same country. As a result of extensive cross-border branching by some banks, the report proposes that national supervisory authorities have the authority to inquire whether the home countries maintain sufficient deposit guarantees that they can protect the deposit of bank branches in host countries. In those cases where the deposit guarantee schemes are not sufficient, the report proposes that national supervisory authorities have the ability to curtail the cross border expansion of banks into their jurisdictions until such deposit guarantees are provided.

The final section of the de Larosiere Report focused on the role of financial sector supervision in the context of highly integrated and interconnected global financial markets in which financial problems can be transmitted quickly around the globe. The report argued that the EU should take a leading role in reforming the international financial architecture by improving its own regulatory and supervisory system. Next, the report argued that the EU should promote international consistency of regulatory standards by strengthening bilateral dialogues on regulation among the main financial centers and by providing a clear mandate for international institutions that determine standards. In particular, the report argues that a strengthened and broadened Financial Stability Forum (now the Financial Stability Board) would be in the best position to coordinate international work on standards. The report also recommended that there should be international colleges of supervisors that can supervise large complex cross-border financial groups. In addition, the Report recommended that central banks should monitor more closely the growth in monetary and credit aggregates and there should be greater macroeconomic surveillance to monitoring macroeconomic policies, exchange rates and global imbalances. In addition to strengthening the IMF 's existing macroeconomic surveillance mechanism, the International Monetary Fund (IMF) and the FSF would be tasked with placing greater emphasis on macro-prudential concerns to provide an early warning system that would be intended to help prevent financial crises. In case another financial crisis should appear, the report recommended that there should be clear multilateral arrangements for coordinating national responses.

Driving European Recovery

"Driving European Recovery," issued by the European Commission (EC), presented a slightly different approach to financial supervision and recovery than that proposed by the de Larosiere group, although it accepts many of the recommendations offered by the group. This approach ultimately was adopted by the EU. The recommendations in the report were intended to complement the economic stimulus measures that were adopted by the EU on November 27, 2008, under the $256 billion Economic Recovery Plan[25] that funded cross-border projects, including investments in clean energy and upgraded telecommunications infrastructure. The plan was meant to ensure that "all relevant actors and all types of financial investments would be subject to appropriate regulation and oversight." In particular, the EC plan noted that nation-based financial supervisory models are lagging behind the market reality of a large number of financial institutions that operate across national borders.

The EC praised the de Larosiere Report for contributing "to a growing consensus about where changes are needed." Of particular interest to the EC were the recommendations to develop a harmonized core set of standards that can be applied throughout the EU. The EC also supported the concept of a new European body similar to the proposed European Systemic Risk Council, but named the European Systemic Risk Board, to gather and assess information on all risks to the financial sector as a whole. It also supported the concept of reforming the current system of EU Committees that oversee the financial sector. The EC plan, however, accelerates the plan proposed by the de Larosiere group by combining the two phases outlined in the report. Using the de Larosiere report as a basis, the EC intends to establish a new European financial supervision system. These efforts to reform the EC's financial supervision system are based on five key objectives:

- First, provide the EU with a supervisory framework that detects potential risks early, deals with them effectively before they have an impact, and meets the challenge of complex international financial markets. The legislative package presented to the European Council, and adopted, includes two elements: measures to establish a European supervision body to oversee the macro- prudential stability of the financial system as a whole; and proposals on the architecture of a European financial supervision system to undertake micro- prudential supervision.
- Second, the EC intends to move to reform those areas where European or national regulation is insufficient or incomplete by proposing a number of items, including: (1) a comprehensive legislative instrument that establishes regulatory and supervisory standards for hedge funds, private equity and other systemically important market players; (2) a White Paper on the necessary tools for early intervention to prevent a similar crisis; (3) measures to increase transparency and ensure financial stability in the area of derivatives and other complex structured products; (4) legislative proposals to increase the quality and quantity of prudential capital for trading book activities and complex securitization; (5) proposals to address liquidity risk and excessive leverage; and (6) a program of actions to establish a more consistent set of supervisory rules.
- Third, to ensure European investors, consumers and small and medium-size enterprises can be confident about their savings, their access to credit and their rights, the EC will: advance a Communication on retail investment products to strengthen the effectiveness of marketing safeguards; provide additional measures to reinforce the protection of bank depositors, investors, and insurance policy holders; and implement measures on responsible lending and borrowing.
- Fourth, in order to improve risk management in financial firms and to align pay incentives with sustainable performance, the EC intends to strengthen the 2004 Recommendation on the remuneration of directors and bring forward a new Recommendation on remuneration in the financial services sector, followed by legislative proposals to include remuneration schemes within the scope of prudential oversight.
- Fifth, to ensure more effective sanctions against market wrongdoing, the EC intends to: review the Market Abuse Directive,[26] and make

proposals on how sanctions could be strengthened in a harmonized manner and better enforced.

CONCLUSION

National authorities are searching for consensus on an international framework to supervise and regulate the complex international financial system. The financial crisis has demonstrated that financial markets are complex, highly integrated and interconnected. At the same time, there are important gaps in the current state of knowledge concerning the nature of the complex linkages that characterize international financial markets. There seems to be some consensus that any new financial architecture should correct the shortcomings of the current system by incorporating a number of features. These features include increased transparency, greater oversight over credit rating firms and underwriting standards, mark-to-market accounting, registration and supervision over hedge funds and other derivative markets, and some supervision of the credit default swap market. Beyond supporting increased supervision over these broad areas of market activities, policymakers remain divided over the specific ways that such supervision should be administered.

Some policymakers also argue that the international financial system can be strengthened through improvements in the data that are collected on financial activities. The Bank of England, for one, argues that the international financial system can benefit from collecting data on the international flow of funds comparable to the U.S. flow of funds accounts. These accounts provide data on financial linkages between domestic and foreign residents and between different parts of the financial sector and the real economy.[27] Policymakers are also focusing on the current size and structure of financial systems in which some institutions have such a far-ranging effect on the financial system that they are deemed to be too big to fail. Policymakers are weighing the benefits of having such firms hold higher amounts of capital and liquidity or limit their activities through regulation or oversight. This issue is particularly pressing for some European countries in which the size of some financial firms is greater than the national GDP and the failure of such firms can be highly destabilizing to the economy.

Furthermore, academics and policymakers are assessing various proposals to address the tendency for the financial system and the real economy to act in a mutually reinforcing, or procyclical, manner. During periods of rapid economic growth and appreciation in the value of assets, the financial markets make credit more readily available, thereby reinforcing the economic boom and the prospects for an asset bubble. Similarly, as an economic boom ends and the real economy begins to slow down, credit markets tighten up, reinforcing the economic contraction. Central banks and policymakers are also focusing on methods and procedures to intervene with banks and other large financial firms that are facing insolvency or failure to provide for an orderly resolution of the firms to maintain market stability. The UK experience with a set of procedures it made permanent in February 2009 may prove useful to some policymakers. The EU acknowledges the importance of this issue, but it has left it up to individual EU members to develop their own approaches.

In the current environment, policymakers and academics also are reconsidering the role central banks play as systemic risk regulators. Central banks acted swiftly to address and contain the financial crisis, which has led some policymakers to weigh the benefits of expanding or amending the role of central banks in the supervision of financial markets. Expanding the role of central banks has some benefits, since central banks generally have the requisite economic resources, the political clout, and the ability to act quickly. Some policymakers, however, question the long-term impact of concentrating market power in an independent agency. In comparing across countries, the statutory role of the central bank is not clear and can vary substantially. As a result, some national governments apparently are considering altering the statutory authority of the central bank to make risk oversight a specific responsibility.

Appendix. Summary of Recommendations of the de Larosiere Report on EU Financial Market Supervision[28]

1. Basel II rules should be amended to: (1) gradually increase minimum capital requirements; (2) reduce pro-cyclicality by encouraging dynamic provisioning of capital buffers; (3) introduce stricter rules for off-balance sheet items; (4) tighten norms on liquidity management; (5) strengthen rules for band internal control and risk management.
2. Adopt a common definition of regulatory capital, including which hybrid instruments should be considered as Tier 1 capital.

3. Relative to regulating credit rating agencies: (1) credit rating agencies should be regulated and supervised by a strengthened Committee of European Securities Regulators (CESR); (2) the credit rating agencies' business model should be reviewed and an assessment should be made of separating rating and advisory activities; (3) the use of ratings in financial regulation should be reduced; (4) distinct codes should be introduced for rating structured products.
4. Mark-to-market accounting rules should be reviewed to: (1) expedite solutions to the remaining accounting issues concerning complex products; (2) ensure they do not bias business models, promote pro-cyclical behavior, or discourage long-term investment; (3) allow the International Accounting Standard Board (IASB) or other standards setting groups clarify and agree on a common, transparent methodology for valuing assets in illiquid markets; (4) have the IASB open its standard-setting process to regulatory, supervisory, and business communities; (5) strengthen the IASB's oversight and governance structure.
5. The Solvency 2 Directive[29] regulations on insurers and reinsurers should be adopted and include a balanced group support regime, coupled with sufficient safeguards for host member states, a binding mediation process between supervisors, and established harmonized insurance guarantee schemes.
6. Competent authorities in all member states must have sufficient supervisory powers, including sanctions, to ensure the compliance of financial institutions with the rules, and they must be equipped with strong, equivalent, and deterrent sanctions to counter all types of financial crimes.
7. Relative to the "parallel banking system" (hedge funds, investment banks, other funds, and mortgage banks): (1) appropriate regulations should be extended to all firms or entities conducting financial activities of a potentially systemic nature; (2) transparency should be improved, especially for systemically important hedge funds; there should be capital requirements on banks owning or operating hedge funds.
8. Securitized products and derivatives markets should: (1) simplify and standardize over-the counter-derivatives; (2) introduce and require the use of at least one well-capitalized central clearing house for credit default swaps in the EU; (3) guarantee that issues of securitized

products retain on their books for the life of the instrument a meaningful amount of the underlying risk.

9. Common rules should be developed for investment funds, including definitions, codification of assets and rules for delegation, accompanied by tighter supervisory control over the independent role of depositories and custodians.
10. Member states and the European Parliament should work toward greater harmonization in rules by avoiding legislation that permits inconsistent transposition and application, and they should identify national exceptions that would improve efficiency by their removal, reduce distortions of competition and regulatory arbitrage, or improve the efficiency of cross-border financial activity in the EU.
11. Compensation incentives must be better aligned with shareholder interests and long-term firm-wide profitability by basing the structure of financial sector compensation schemes on the following principles: (1) bonuses should be set in a multi-year framework; (2) the same set of rules should be applied to proprietary traders and asset managers; and (3) bonuses should reflect actual performance and not be guaranteed in advance.
12. Internal risk management should be: independent and responsible for effective, independent stress testing; senior risk officers should hold a very high rank in the company; and internal risk assessment and proper due diligence must not be neglected by overreliance on external ratings.
13. The EU should have a coherent and workable regulatory framework for crisis management; a framework that is transparent; the relevant authorities should be equipped with appropriate and equivalent crisis prevention and crisis management tools; and legal obstacles that prevent the use of these tools in a cross-border crisis should be removed.
14. Deposit Guarantee Schemes should be harmonized and prefunded by the private sector and provide high, equal protection to all bank customers throughout the EU; the schemes should protect all customers; and the existing authorities of host countries regarding cross-border bank branches should be reviewed.
15. Member states should agree on more detailed criteria for burden sharing (providing financial aid from the public and private sector) than those contained in existing agreements.

16. The EU should create a new body called the European Systemic Risk Council (ESRC) to pool and analyze all information, relevant for financial stability, pertaining to macro-economic conditions and to macro-prudential developments in all the financial sectors.
17. The EU should put in place an early warning system under the auspices of the ESRC and of the Economic and Financial Committee (EFC) to: (1) prioritize and issue macro-prudential risk warnings; (2) direct risks that potentially could affect the financial sector or the economy to the EFC to implement a strategy to address those risks; (3) warn the IMF, the FSF, and the BIS if risks relate to global dysfunction of the monetary and financial system; and (4) take additional action if the response of a national supervisor is inadequate.
18. A European System of Financial Supervisors (ESFS) should be established to: (1) work with the existing national supervisors who would continue to carry out day- to-day supervision; (2) replace three existing structures (Committee of European Banking Supervisors (CEBS), Committee of European Insurance and Occupational Pensions Supervisors (CEIOPS), and the Committee of European Securities Regulators (CESR) with three new European Authorities tasked with coordinating supervisory standards and guaranteeing strong cooperation between national supervisors; also (3) colleges of supervisors should be established for all major cross-border institutions.
19. National supervisory authorities should be strengthened to upgrade the quality of supervision, including: (1) reforming national systems by aligning supervisors' competences and powers on a comprehensive system in the EU, increasing supervisors' remuneration, facilitating exchanges of personnel between the private sector and supervisory authorities, and ensuring that all supervisory authorities implement a modern and attractive personnel policy; and (2) intensifying the training and personnel exchanges of the level 3 committees; carrying out an examination of the degree of independence of all national supervisors.
20. The EU should develop a more harmonized set of financial regulations, supervisory powers, and sanctioning regimes.
21. The level 3 committees (national regulators) should: (1) gain a significant increase in their resources; (2) upgrade the quality and impact of peer review processes; (3) prepare for establishing

supervisory colleges[30] for all major cross- border financial firms in the EU by the end of 2009.

22. The EU should establish an integrated European System of Financial Supervision (ESFS) and the level 3 committees should be transformed into three European Authorities – a European Banking Authority, a European Insurance Authority, and a European Securities Authority – with boards comprised of the chairs of the national supervisory authorities and have their own autonomous budget and a set of key competencies that include: legally binding mediation between national supervisors; adoption of binding supervisory standards; and binding technical decisions applicable to individual financial institutions.
23. Planning for an integrated European System of Financial Supervision should begin immediately with a detailed plan for implementation developed before the end of 2009.
24. The ESFS should be reviewed within three years of its implementation and additional reforms considered.
25. The Financial Stability Board should be in charge of promoting the convergence of international financial regulation to the highest benchmarks, the Board should be enlarged, it should report to the IMF, and it should be transformed into a decision-making Council.
26. Supervisory colleges for large complex, cross-border financial groups should carry out robust, comprehensive risk assessments, should pay greater attention to banks' internal risk management practices and should agree on a common approach to aligning incentives in private sector remuneration schemes.
27. The IMF should be placed in charge of developing and operating a financial stability early warning system, accompanied by an international risk map and credit register.
28. Efforts should be intensified to encourage jurisdictions that currently are poorly regulated or "uncooperative" to adhere to the highest level of international standard and to exchange information among supervisors. Supervisors should increase capital requirements for those financial institutions that are investing in or doing business with poorly regulated jurisdictions.
29. EU members should show their support for strengthening the role of the IMF in macroeconomic surveillance and to contribute towards increasing the IMF 's resources in order to strengthen its capacity to support member countries facing acute financial or balance of payment distress.

30. The EU should organize itself so it can represent itself in a coherent manner in the new global economic and financial architecture.
31. In its bilateral relations, the EU should intensify its financial regulatory dialogue with key partners.

End Notes

[1] Members of the euro area are Austria, Belgium, Cyprus, Finland, France, Germany, Greece, Ireland, Italy, Luxembourg, Malta, the Netherlands, Portugal, Slovakia, Slovenia, and Spain.

[2] Members of the European Union are: Austria, Belgium, Bulgaria, Cyprus, the Czech Republic, Denmark, Estonia, Finland, France, Germany, Greece, Hungary, Republic of Ireland, Italy, Latvia, Lithuania, Luxembourg, Malta, the Netherlands, Poland, Portugal, Romania, Slovakia, Slovenia, Sweden, and the United Kingdom.

[3] The Stability and Growth Pact (SGP) is an agreement by European Union members to conduct their fiscal policy in a manner that facilitates and maintains the Economic and Monetary Union of the European Union. The Pact was adopted in 1997 and is based on Articles 99 and 104 of the European Community Treaty, or the Maastricht Treaty, and related decisions. It consists of monitoring the fiscal policies of the members by the European Commission and the Council so that fiscal discipline is maintained and enforced in the Economic and Monetary Union (EMU). The actual criteria that members states must respect are: (1) an annual budget deficit no higher than 3% of GDP, and (2) a national debt lower than 60% of GDP, or approaching that value.

[4] The Lisbon Strategy for Growth and Jobs is a plan adopted by EU members to improve economic growth and employment among the EU members by becoming the most competitive knowledge based economy in the world by 2010. The comprehensive strategy includes adopting sustainable macroeconomic policies, business friendly regulatory and tax policies and benefits, improved education and training, and greater investment in energy efficient and environmentally friendly technology. Two major goals include total public and private investment of 3% of Europe's GDP in research and employment by 2010, and an employment rate of 70% by the same date. A comprehensive report on the Lisbon Strategy is available at: http://ec.europa.EU/growthandjobs/pdf/kok_report_en.pdf.

[5] The Financial Services Action Plan replaced the Investment Services Directive and contains a set of measures that are intended to remove the remaining formal barriers in the financial services market among EU members and to provide a legal and regulatory environment that supports the integration of the EU financial markets. *The EU Financial Services Action Plan: A Guide*, HM Treasury, the Financial Services authority, and the Bank of England, July 31, 2003.

[6] *EU Banking Structures*, European Central Bank, October 2008.

[7] Davies, Ryan J., *MiFID and a Changing Competitive Landscape*, July 2008, p. 3; available at *http://faculty.babson*. edu/rdavies/ MiFID_July2008_Davies15.pdf.

[8] *The EU Financial Services Action Plan: A Guide*, HM Treasury, the Financial Services Authority, and the Bank of England, July 31, 2003.

[9] Basel II is the second of the Basel Accords, which are recommendations on banking laws and regulations issued by the Basel Committee on Banking Supervision. The purpose of Basel II is to create an international standard that banking regulators can use when creating regulations concerning requirements for capital adequacy that banks must meet to guard against the types of financial and operational risks that banks face.

[10] National Supervisors are one or more supervisory authorities that are authorized at the national level and are accountable to national mechanisms to issue regulations, grant licenses, conduct supervision, and to take enforcement action.

[11] The Lamfalussy process, named after Alesandre Lamfalussy who chaired the EU advisory committee that created it, was adopted by the EU members in 1999 to accelerate the legislative process in the EU relative to financial services legislation in order to meet the implementation deadline of the financial Services Action Plan by 2005. The process is composed of four levels, each focusing on a specific stage in the implementation of legislation with the EU. Level I establishes the core values of a law and is the traditional EU decision making, in which decisions are adopted as Directives or Regulations proposed by the Commission and then approved under the co-decision procedure by the European Parliament and the EU Council. At the second level, sector-specific committees and regulators provide advice on developing the technical details of the principles that were adopted in Level I. At the third level, national regulators work on coordinating new regulations with other nations. The fourth level involves compliance and enforcement. This process is intended to promote consistent interpretation, convergence in national supervisory practices, and an improvement in the quality of legislation on financial services.

[12] Hardy, Daniel, A "European Mandate" for Financial Sector Authorities in the EU, in *Euro Area Policies: Selected Issues*, the International Monetary Fund, IMF Country Report No. 08/263, August 2008.

[13] *From Financial Crisis to Recovery: A European Framework for Action*, Communication From the Commission, European Commission, COM(2008) 706 final, October 29, 2008.

[14] The Lisbon Strategy for Growth and Jobs is a plan adopted by EU members to improve economic growth and employment among the EU members by becoming the most competitive knowledge based economy in the world by 2010. The comprehensive strategy includes adopting sustainable macroeconomic policies, business friendly regulatory and tax policies and benefits, improved education and training, and greater investment in energy efficient and environmentally friendly technology. Two major goals include total public and private investment of 3% of Europe's GDP in research and employment by 2010, and an employment rate of 70% by the same date. A comprehensive report on the Lisbon Strategy is available at: http://ec.europa.eu/growthandjobs/pdf/kok_report_en.pdf

[15] The combination of labor market flexibility and security for workers.

[16] The Stability and Growth Pact (SGP) is an agreement by European Union members to conduct their fiscal policy in a manner that facilitates and maintains the Economic and Monetary Union of the European Union. The Pact was adopted in 1997 and is based on Articles 99 and 104 of the European Community Treaty, or the Maastricht Treaty, and related decisions. It consists of monitoring the fiscal policies of the members by the European Commission and the Council so that fiscal discipline is maintained and enforced in the European Monetary Union (EMU). The actual criteria that member states must respect are (1) an annual budget deficit no higher than 3% of GDP, and (2) a national debt lower than 60% of GDP or approaching that value.

[17] The European Social Fund, created in 1957, is the EU's main financial instrument for assisting members in implementing their own plans for investing in workers.

[18] *Report*, The High-Level Group on Financial Supervision in the EU, Chaired by Jacques de Larosiere, February 25, 2009.

[19] *Driving European Recovery*, Communication for the Spring European Council, Commission of the European Communities, April 3, 2009.

[20] *Report*, The High-Level Group on Financial Supervision in the EU, Chaired by Jacques de Larosiere, February 25, 2009, p. 10.

[21] Ibid., p. 11.

[22] Level 3 committees represent the third level of the Lamfalussy process the EU uses to implement EU-wide policies. At the third level, national regulators work on coordinating new regulations with other nations, and they may adopt non-binding guidelines or common

standards regarding matters not covered by EU legislation, as long as these standards are compatible with the legislation adopted at Level 1 and Level 2.

[23] The European System of Central Banks is comprised of the European Central Bank, which represents those countries that have joined the Euro area, and the central banks of all of the members of the European Union.

[24] These functions include: advising the European Commission on regulatory and other issues, defining overall supervisory policies, convergence of supervisory rules and practices, financial stability monitoring, and oversight of supervisory colleges.

[25] *A European Economic Recovery Plan*: Communication From the Commission to the European Council, Commission of the European Communities, COM(2008) 800 final, November 26, 2008. The full report is available at http://ec.europa.eu/commission_ barroso/ president/ pdf/Comm_20081126.pdf

[26] The Market Abuse Directive was adopted by the European Commission in April 2004. The Directive is intended to reinforce market integrity in the EU and contribute to the harmonization of the rules against market abuse and establishing transparency and equal treatment of market participants in such areas as accepted market practices in the context of market manipulation, the definition of inside information relative to derivatives on commodities, and the notification of the relevant authorities of suspicious transactions.

[27] *Financial Stability Report*, The Bank of England, June 2009, p. 46.

[28] *Report*, The High-Level Group on Financial Supervision in the EU, Chaired by Jacques de Larosiere, February 25, 2009.

[29] The Solvency II Directive attempts by 2012 to bring insurers and reinsurers under the same regulatory regime that will provide a single set of rules that govern what constitutes an acceptable level of insurer creditworthiness.

[30] Supervisory colleges are intended to be a formal structure that brings together the relevant national authorities under a lead supervisor to coordinate policies on cross-border financial activities.

In: International Perspectives on Financial... ISBN: 978-1-61728-006-1
Editor: James P. Corrigan © 2011 Nova Science Publishers, Inc.

Chapter 3

FINANCIAL MARKET SUPERVISION: CANADA'S PERSPECTIVE*

James K. Jackson

SUMMARY

The international financial crisis has spurred policymakers in the United States and elsewhere to consider changing the way they currently supervise financial institutions and financial markets to reduce the prospects of experiencing another global financial crisis. Canada's financial system, in particular is garnering attention, because it seems to be more resistant to the failures and bailouts that have marked banks in the United States and Europe. In particular, some observers are assessing the merits of the way Canada supervises and regulates its banks, as one possible model for the United States. There likely are aspects of Canada's financial supervisory framework that may offer an approach to supervising financial markets that may be useful for the United States to consider. However, the smaller scope of Canada's financial system and its economy likely lessen the transferability of systems or procedures used in Canada to the vastly more complex U.S. financial system. This chapter presents an overview of Canada's financial system and its

* This is an edited, reformatted and augmented version of a CRS Report for Congress publication dated November 2009.

supervisory framework and draws some distinctions between that system and the current U.S. framework.

BACKGROUND

The current financial crisis is prompting U.S. and foreign leaders to search for national models that have proven superior in supervising and regulating financial markets and for a new international order that can help mitigate any recurrence of the crisis. Canada's financial system, in particular, is garnering, attention because it seems to be more resistant during the crisis to the failures and bailouts that have marked banks in the United States and Europe. In particular, some observers are assessing the merits of Canada's financial system, especially the way it supervises and regulates its banks, as one possible model for the United States. Currently, advanced economies employ a number of institutional structures to supervise and regulate their financial sectors.

No single model of market supervision has proven to be clearly superior, but the trend seems to be toward more integrated arrangements. Reportedly, the Obama administration considered at one time replacing the multiple agencies that supervise and regulate the U.S. financial system with a single regulator.[1] It has proposed instead changes to the existing system that enhances the role of the Federal Reserve and creates two new agencies and a new Financial Services Oversight Council.[2] Members of Congress are likely to propose alternative approaches to reordering the supervision of U.S. financial markets. A number of countries have opted for a twin peaks approach where prudential regulation (focusing on the long-term view of market performance) is assigned to one regulator and market conduct regulation (focusing on the day-to-day operation of the market) to another. Great Britain employs a different model where there is a fully unified regulator that is separate from the central bank. Others, like the United States, have opted for specialized federal regulators, while reserving a role for state regulators in securities regulation. Canada's model assigns the central bank the main role of conducting monetary policy and maintaining price stability. It has assigned the core responsibility for supervising and regulating some aspects of the financial system to a separate federal agency, while also giving provincial governments authority over other parts of the financial system.

While Canada has not injected capital directly into its banks to forestall a failure, the financial crisis and global economic recession are battering the Canadian economy in ways that are similar to those in the United States and in Europe. The International Monetary Fund (IMF) recently forecast that the Canadian economy, as represented by gross domestic product (GDP), could contract by 2.5% in 2009, before rebounding with a positive rate of economic growth of 1.2% in 2010, as indicated in Table 1. The Bank of Canada, however, projected that the Canadian economy would contract by 3.0% in 2009, and then rebound in 2010 at a 2.5% annual rate of growth.[3] In comparison, the U.S. economy is forecast to decline by 2.8% in 2009 and remain flat in 2010.[4] The IMF forecast also indicates that unemployment in Canada will rise to 8.4% in 2009 and 8.8% in 2010. The slowdown in economic growth, in large part, reflects Canada's vulnerability to spillover effects from the U.S. economy, since three-fourths of Canada's exports are bound for the United States and about one-fourth of Canadian corporate finance is sourced there.[5] Canadian exports of automotive products, forest products, and industrial materials posted steep declines in the first quarter of 2009, and Canadian firms cut about 270,000 jobs in the first quarter and reduced the average work week.[6] The slowdown was especially pronounced in the first quarter of 2009, when GDP fell by 7.1%, according to the Bank of Canada.[7] Canadian banks are also expected to face a number of challenges over the next year that include a continued contraction in output, falling household incomes, and rising unemployment. Although Canadian credit markets have improved over the first half of 2009, certain markets for asset backed securities (ABS) remain frozen. The Bank of Canada indicated in June 2009 that the number of such securities had fallen by about 20% since June 2007, because maturing securities are not being replaced by new issues.[8] The IMF has indicated that Canada is generally better situated than many other countries to weather the financial crisis and the global economic downturn. This resilience can be attributed to three factors. First, Canada positioned itself well prior to the financial crisis through a conservative macroeconomic policy that reduced the federal government's debt relative to GDP and through a relatively tight monetary policy that focused on price stability.[9]

Secondly, the IMF argues that Canadian banks have performed better, because Canadian authorities acted proactively in addressing the potential economic slowdown. They did this by: 1) adopting a major fiscal stimulus of Can$65 billion on October 30, 2008; 2) adopting an additional fiscal stimulus program in early January 2009; and 3) easing monetary policy through a series of cuts in key interest rates. As part of Canada's Economic Action Plan adopted in January 2009, officials implemented additional policy measures they can employ should further actions be necessary. The economic plan comprises five elements: 1) funding for job and skills training; 2) funding to stimulate housing construction; 3) investment in infrastructure; 4) support for major export sectors, including automotive, forestry, and manufacturing; and 5) improving access to financing through the Extraordinary Financing Framework. In the early stages of the financial crisis, the Bank of Canada also provided liquidity by expanding its liquidity facilities and the Government of Canada purchased some insured mortgages through the Canada Mortgage and Housing Corporation.[10]

Table 1. Canada's Actual and Projected Real GDP, Consumer Prices, and Rate of Unemployment (Annual percentage changes and percent of labor force)

	2007	2008	2009	2010
	Actual		Projected	
Real GDP	2.7%	0.5%	-2.5%	1.2%
Consumer Prices	2.1	2.4	0.0	0.5
Unemployment	6.0	6.2	8.4	8.8

Source: *World Economic Outlook*, International Monetary Fund, April, 2009.

In addition, the Extraordinary Financing Framework is comprised of five elements: 1) providing funding to Canadian financial institutions through the Insured Mortgage Purchase Program and the Canada Mortgage Bond program; 2) expanding financing for Canadian businesses through Export Development Canada and the Business Development Bank of Canada; 3) increasing collaboration between financial Crown corporations[11] and private sector lenders and credit insurers under a business Credit Availability program; 4) designing a Canadian Secured Credit Facility; and 5) initiating a Canadian Lenders Assurance Facility and the Canadian Life Insurers Assurance Facility to provide insurance on the wholesale term borrowing of federally regulated deposit-taking institutions, and life insurers. Additional measures include the ability to offer guarantees on bank and insurance liabilities, and the authority to engage in transactions to maintain financial stability, including providing capital injections.[12]

Finally, the IMF argues that financial conditions have remained more favorable in Canada, because Canadian banks are managed conservatively. Canadian banks are required to maintain larger capital requirements than elsewhere, which has meant that Canadian banks had a stronger balance sheet position as the crisis developed. The regulatory structure also discourages Canadian banks from taking excessive risks. This system is centered around two key thresholds: minimum risk-based capital ratios; and a maximum assets-to-capital multiple. Canada requires banks to hold capital at rates that are higher than those set in the Basel Accords; Canada requires its banks to hold tier 1 capital[13] of at least 7% and total capital of 10%, compared with 4% and 8%, respectively, for the Basel Accord. In addition, Canada requires that 75% of the tier 1 capital be in the form of common equity and it restricts innovative instruments to 15% of tier 1 capital. In addition, the assets-to-capital multiple is set at 20, which translates into a leverage ratio of 5%. The capital requirements not only provide an enhanced capital cushion for Canadian banks, but they restrict rapid balance sheet expansion and discourage engaging in wholesale operations.[14] Nevertheless, as the financial crisis unfolded, the banks came under pressure from markets to increase their capital ratios, which they apparently did by tapping private sources.[15] In addition, the IMF points out that Canadian banks have been more resilient, because Canada has a strong financial regulatory and supervisory framework.[16]

As a result of these three factors, no Canadian bank has needed public capital injections and none have used public guarantees.[17] Nevertheless, the banks suffered a loss of 50% in the value of their equities, similar to the experience of such equities in the United States and Europe. The Canadian Imperial Bank of Commerce lost $2.1 billion in derivatives in 2008. The drop in commodity prices also caused the Canadian dollar to fall relative to the U.S. dollar, which would improve the cost competitive position of Canada's exports, once a recovery begins. As the recovery begins, however, demand for raw materials will increase, which, in turn, will cause the Canadian dollar to appreciate. At the present time, the slowdown in global trade, the shake-out in the auto industry, and a slowdown in exports of construction-related products are having far-reaching negative effects on the Canadian economy. In January, 2009, the Canadian Government announced about a Can$40 billion fiscal stimulus package over two years in infrastructure spending, tax decreases, worker retraining, housing, and aid to struggling industries to spur the Canadian economy, as indicated in Table 2. The stimulus to the Canadian economy provided by this economic package is expected to be supplemented by spending by the provincial governments. In addition, on April 21, 2009, the Bank of Canada lowered the nation's key interest rate to 0.25%.

Table 2. Canada's Economic Action Plan (in millions of Canadian dollars)

	2009	2010	Total
Action to Help Canadians and Stimulate Spending	$5.880	$6.945	$1 2.825
Action to Stimulate Housing Construction	5,365	2,395	7,760
Housing leverage	725	750	1,475
Immediate Action to Build Infrastructure	6,224	5,605	11,829
Infrastructure leverage	4,532	4,365	8,897
Action to Support Businesses and Communities	5,272	2,255	7,527
Sectoral leverage	1,300		1,300
Total Federal Stimulus	22,742	17,200	39,942
Total Stimulus (with leverage)	29,298	22,316	51,613
Total Stimulus as a share of GDP (%)	1.5	1.1	2.5
Total Stimulus (with leverage) as a share of GDP (%)	1.9	1.4	3.2

Source: Canada's Economic Action Plan, 2009 Budget, Chapter 3, Ministry of Finance.

A recent IMF staff report used three measures to assess the financial strength of Canada's banks as a way of understanding the relative success the banks experienced in avoiding the same intensity of financial troubles that afflicted banks in other major economies. These measures include: 1) capital-assets ratios (total equity divided by total assets), since better-capitalized banks likely can sustain higher losses without becoming insolvent; 2) balance sheet liquidity (total liquid assets divided by total liabilities), because a buffer of liquid assets allows banks to cover transitory cash-flow shortfalls; and 3) the funding structure of the banks, or the share of their funding that is derived from deposits, since deposit insurance likely improves the stability of this source of funding. The results of the measures are presented in Table 3, Table 4, and Table 5. The three tables also include a measure of the percentage decline from January 2007 to January 2009 in the value of the equity of the individual banks. They also provide some basic information on the nature of any government intervention that was needed to assist the individual banks.

Table 3, Table 4, and Table 5 indicate that Canadian banks are not exceptionally financially strong relative to banks in other OECD countries. In some cases, the capital ratios of Canadian banks were half or less than that of a number of U.S. firms that experienced significant liquidity problems as the financial crisis progressed. Similarly, Canadian banks did not have balance sheet liquidity that was significantly different from that of other banks. As indicated by the IMF report, and as indicated in Table 5 the major difference between Canadian banks and banks in other OECD countries is the funding source of those banks. Canadian banks generally relied much less on wholesale funding, or borrowing short-term from money markets. Instead, the banks relied on depository funding, much of which came from such retail sources as households, for a higher share of their funding.[18] This success in attracting household deposits may in part stem from the ability of Canadian banks, as universal banks, to offer one-stop service in mutual funds and asset management. [19]

Table 3. Capital Ratios of Major Banks

Bank	Country	Capital Ratio	Value decline	Intervention
Hypo Real Estate Holding AG	Germany	2.1	97%	Asset guarantees and public loans
Deutsche Bank AG	Germany	2.1	81	
UBS AG	Switzerland	2.3	79	Capital injection
Commerzbank AG	Germany	2.5	89	Capital injection
ABN Amro Holding NV	Netherlands	2.6	NA	Nationalized (carved out from Fortis)
Barclays Plc	United Kingdom	2.7	85	
Fortis	Belgium	2.8	94	Broken up, part nationalized
Dresdner Bank AG	Germany	3.0	NA	Capital injection
Northern Rock Plc	United Kingdom	3.2	100	Nationalized
Dexia	Belgium	3.3	89	Nationalized
ING Groep NV	Netherlands	3.3	81	Recapitalized, asset guarantees
Lloyds TSB Group Plc	United Kingdom	3.3	78	Capital injection
HBOS Plc	United Kingdom	3.6	100	Recapitalized (part of Lloyds)
Canadian Imperial Bank of Commerce	Canada	4.1	54	
Royal Bank of Canada RBC	Canada	4.3	44	
Credit Suisse Group	Switzerland	4.7	66	
Banque de Montreal-Bank of Montreal	Canada	4.8	53	

Table 3. (Continued)

Bank	Country	Capital Ratio	Value decline	Intervention
Bank of Nova Scotia (The)	Canada	4.9	42	
Royal Bank of Scotland Group Plc (The)	United Kingdom	5.2	96	Capital injection, asset guarantees
Westpac Banking Corporation	Australia	5.3	38	
Commonwealth Bank of Australia	Australia	5.7	46	
National Australia Bank	Australia	5.7	53	
Toronto Dominion Bank	Canada	5.7	43	
Australia and New Zealand Banking Group	Australia	5.9	54	
Citigroup Inc	USA	6.4	94	Recapitalized, asset guarantees
HSBC Holdings Plc	United Kingdom	6.6	41	
Washington Mutual Inc.	USA	8.5	100	Failed, taken over by FDIC
JP Morgan Chase & Co.	USA	8.6	50	
Bank of America Corporation	USA	9.3	87	Capital injection, asset guarantees
Wells Fargo & Company	USA	9.5	47	
Wachovia Corporation	USA	10.3	100	Failed, acquired by Wells Fargo
Capital One Financial Corporation	USA	16.9	80	

Source: Ratnovski, Lev, and Rocco Huang, *Why Are Canadian Banks More Resilient?,* IMF Working Paper WP/09/152, International Monetary Fund, July 2009.

Note: Capital represents bank equity divided by total assets. Value decline is a measure of the percentage decline from January 2007 to January 2009 in the value of the equity of the respective bank. Intervention represents some basic information about the nature of any government intervention.

Table 4. Balance Sheet Liquidity of Major Banks

Bank	Country	Liquidity	Value decline	Intervention
Capital One Financial Corporation	USA	3.70%	80%	
National City Corporation	USA	4.00	100	Acquired by PNC Bank
Citizens Financial Group Inc.	USA	4.30	NA	NA (owned by RBS)
SunTrust Banks, Inc.	USA	4.30	85	
US Bancorp	USA	4.40	58	
Washington Mutual Inc.	USA	4.80	100	Failed, taken over by FDIC
Regions Financial	USA	5.00	90	
Corporation				
Nomura Holdings Inc	JAPAN	5.60	76	
Wells Fargo & Company	USA	6.00	47	
Northern Rock Plc	United Kingdom	6.70	100	Nationalized
Kookmin Bank	Korea	7.80	56	
Bank of Ireland	Ireland	8.40	96	Capital injection, liabilities guarantee
Commonwealth Bank of Australia	Australia	8.90	46	
Australia and New Zealand Banking Group	Australia	10.32	54	
Westpac Banking Corporation	Australia	10.42	38	
Wachovia Corporation	USA	10.69	100	Failed, acquired by Wells Fargo
HBOS Plc	United Kingdom	11.14	100	Capital injection (part of Lloys)
National Australia Bank	Australia	11.15		
Lloyds TSB Group Plc	United Kingdom	15.67	78	Capital injection

Table 4. (continued)

Bank	Country	Liquidity	Value decline	Intervention
Banque de Montreal-Bank of Montreal	Canada	23.99	53	
Toronto Dominion Bank	Canada	24.37	43	
Bank of Nova Scotia (The)	Canada	24.43	42	
Royal Bank of Scotland Group Plc (The)	United Kingdom	25.11	96	Capital injection, asset guarantees
Bank of America Corporation	USA	25.59	87	Capital injection, asset guarantees
Canadian Imperial Bank of Commerce	Canada	26.00	54	
Royal Bank of Canada RBC	Canada	32.11	44	
HSBC Holdings Plc	United Kingdom	33.20	41	
Citigroup Inc	USA	39.46	94	Recapitalized, asset guarantees
Barclays Plc	United Kingdom	40.75	85	
JP Morgan Chase & Co.	USA	46.80	50	
Credit Suisse Group	Switzerland	64.93	66	
UBS AG	Switzerland	65.20	79	Capital injection

Source: Ratnovski, Lev, and Rocco Huang, *Why Are Canadian Banks More Resilient?,* IMF Working Paper WP/09/152, International Monetary Fund, July 2009.

Note: Liquidity represents total liquid assets divided by total liabilities. Value decline is a measure of the percentage decline from January 2007 to January 2009 in the value of the equity of the respective bank. Intervention represents some basic information about the nature of any government intervention.

Table 5. Depository Funding of Major Banks

Bank	Country	Depository funding	Value decline	Intervention
Hypo Real Estate Holding AG	Germany	24.0%	97%	Asset guarantees and public loans
Northern Rock Plc	United	28.7	100	Nationalized

	Kingdom			
Deutsche Bank AG	Germany	34.1	81	
BNP Paribas	France	36.7	65	
Citigroup Inc	USA	37.8	94	Capital injection, asset guarantees
HBOS Plc	United Kingdom	41.0	100	Capital injection (part of Lloyds)
Société Générale	France	42.0	74	
Banca Monte dei Paschi di Siena SpA	Italy	44.1	68	
Dexia	Belgium	44.9	89	Nationalized
DnB Nor ASA	Norway	45.4	74	
Danske Bank A/S	Denmark	46.3	78	
Commerzbank AG	Germany	47.0	89	Capital injection
JP Morgan Chase & Co.	USA	47.3	50	
Barclays Plc	United Kingdom	47.7	85	
Bank of America Corporation	USA	47.9	87	Capital injection, asset guarantees
National Australia Bank	Australia	51.7	53	
Commonwealth Bank of Australia	Australia	53.4	46	
HSBC Holdings Plc	United Kingdom	54.9	41	
Credit Suisse Group	Switzerland	55.6	66	
Capital One Financial Corporation	USA	57.3	80	
Lloyds TSB Group Plc	United Kingdom	58.7	78	Capital injection
Royal Bank of Scotland Group Plc (The)	United Kingdom	59.3	96	Capital injection, asset guarantees
Wachovia Corporation	USA	62.8	100	Failed, acquired by Wells Fargo
UBS AG	Switzerland	64.1	79	Capital injection
Wells Fargo & Company	USA	64.4	47	
Royal Bank of Canada RBC	Canada	65.1	44	
Banque de Montreal-Bank of Montreal	Canada	65.2	53	
Australia and New Zealand Banking Group	Australia	65.4	54	
Toronto Dominion Bank	Canada	67.9	43	

Table 5. (Continued)

Bank	Country	Depository funding	Value decline	Intervention
Canadian Imperial Bank of Commerce	Canada	68.2	54	
Bank of Nova Scotia (The)	Canada	71.4	42	
Westpac Banking Corporation	Australia	74.1	38	
Washington Mutual Inc.	USA	74.6	100	Failed, taken over by FDIC

Source: Ratnovski, Lev, and Rocco Huang, *Why Are Canadian Banks More Resilient?,* IMF Working Paper WP/09/152, International Monetary Fund, July 2009.

Note: Depository funding represents the share of total bank funding that is derived from deposits. Value decline is a measure of the percentage decline from January 2007 to January 2009 in the value of the equity of the respective bank. Intervention represents some basic information about the nature of any government intervention.

THE U.S. FINANCIAL SUPERVISORY SYSTEM

Currently, the United States has a complex regulatory framework in which agencies have overlapping jurisdiction, and in which there are some regulatory gaps.[20] Congress and the Administration are considering a number of changes to the supervisory framework in an effort to improve the system and to correct weaknesses. Not all of the regulators have the authority to address systemic risk, and no single regulator has jurisdiction over all the financial institutions and markets. As indicated in **Figure 1**, financial supervision can be separated into three main categories: supervision of banks, supervision of non-banks, and those markets that are unregulated. For ease of presentation, the figure shows only the major lines of supervisory responsibility. For instance, the President nominates the Governors of the Federal Reserve Board, but the Treasury Department closely coordinates with the Federal Reserve in developing and implementing policy. The Chairman of the Federal Reserve, however, formally reports to Congress, so the figure shows only this line of responsibility. Similarly, the Administration coordinates closely with many of the other independent agencies that supervise parts of the financial system.

The U.S. financial system is also characterized by a combination of federally chartered financial institutions and financial institutions chartered by the individual 50 States. This system, some observers argue, has allowed banks that faced federal regulatory action to walk away from federal regulators and move under state supervision by converting their charters to a state charter.[21] National banks are supervised by the Office of the Comptroller of the Currency that is under the direction of the U.S. Treasury Department. The Office of Thrift Supervision, also within the Treasury Department, supervises State and federally chartered thrift institutions. Next, the U.S. Congress has established a number of independent agencies that supervise various parts of the financial system. These agencies include the Federal Deposit Insurance Corporation that directly supervises State banks that are not part of the Federal Reserve System and indirectly supervises State and federally chartered thrifts and State banks, such as commercial banks and industrial banks. Next, the Federal Reserve System is the central bank of the United States and is comprised of the Board of Governors and 12 District Federal Reserve Banks. These banks supervise all State banks that are part of the Federal Reserve System, bank holding companies, the foreign activities of member banks, the U.S. activities of foreign banks, and Edge Act, or limited-purpose institutions that engage in foreign banking business. The National Credit Union Administration supervises the many credit unions. In addition to these federal entities, State entities supervise State chartered thrifts and State banks.

In the area of non-bank supervision, the U.S. Congress has chartered three independent agencies. These agencies include the Securities and Exchange Commission, which supervises all securities trading and securities firms, the Commodity Futures Trading Commission, which supervises the trading of commodities, and the Federal Housing Finance Agency, which supervises the Federal National Mortgage Association (Fannie Mae), the Federal Home Loan Mortgage Association (Freddie Mac), and the Federal Home Loan Banks. State agencies also regulate and supervise insurance activities. Beyond this area of supervision, there is a broad group of financial activities that have not been directly supervised, including the rapidly growing area of derivatives trading.

On June 17, 2009, President Obama presented his plan for overhauling supervision of the financial services sector. Prospects for the plan are uncertain, since Members of Congress likely will propose alternative approaches to reordering the supervision of the U.S. financial markets. The Obama Administration's plan has a number of components. First, the Federal Reserve would gain the authority to supervise any large firm, regardless of which specific sector of the financial markets the firm is involved with, if the Treasury had determined that the firm poses a threat to the overall financial system. The Fed could also require such firms to hold more reserves and to take fewer risks. This proposal would significantly broaden the supervisory reach of the Federal Reserve over its current responsibilities. Next, the proposal would create a new Financial Services Oversight Council that would be chaired by the Department of the Treasury and include the heads of the principal federal financial regulators.

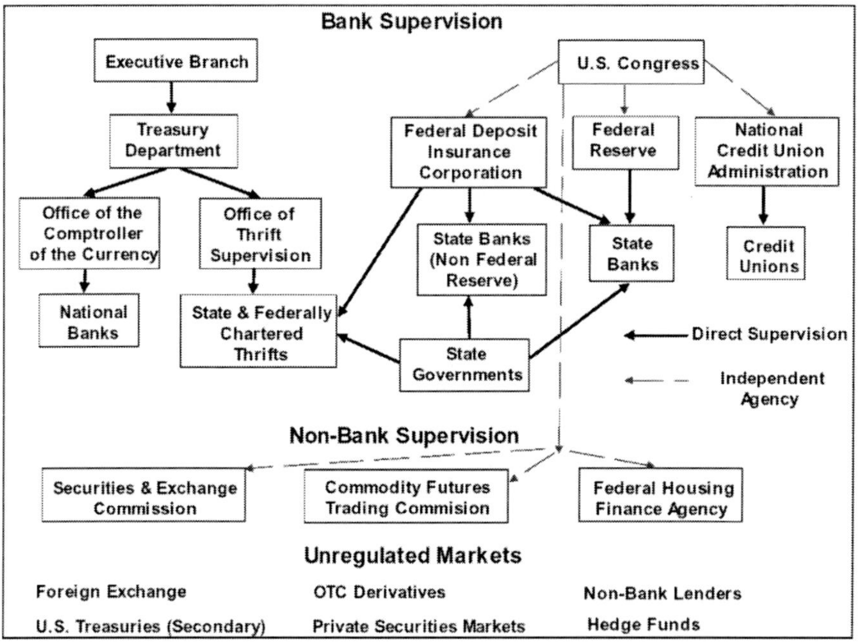

Source: Developed by CRS.

Figure 1. U.S. System for Supervising Financial Markets

Third, President Obama's plan would create the Consumer Financial Protection Agency, which would set and enforce regulations regarding consumer loans, including credit cards and mortgages. Fourth, the plan would create a new National Bank Supervisor to replace the Office of the Comptroller of the Currency (OCC) and the Office of Thrift Supervision (OTS). Fifth, the plan would give the Federal Deposit Insurance Corporation (FDIC) the authority to take over and shut down financial institutions whose failure would threaten the stability of the financial system. Sixth, the Commodities Futures Trading Commission and the Securities and Exchange Commission would have more authority to regulate derivatives. Finally, the

Securities and Exchange Commission would also gain the authority to supervise hedge funds and mutual funds.

On March 23, 2009, Senator Collins introduced S. 664, the Financial System Stabilization and Reform Act of 2009. A companion measure, H.R. 1754, was introduced in the House of Representatives by Representative Castle. These proposals would create a Financial Stability Council that would be chaired by an individual appointed by the President and confirmed by the Senate, with the Secretary of the Treasury, the Chairman of the Federal Reserve Board, the Chairman of the FDIC, the chairman of the National Credit Union Administration, the Chairman of the Securities and Exchange Commission, and the chairman of the Commodities Future Trading Commission serving as members of the Council. In addition, the Federal Reserve would be granted authority to examine the soundness and safety of the financial system posed by bank holding companies.

In addition, the Securities and Exchange Commission would be required to designate a clearinghouse for credit default swaps and to prohibit "fraudulent, deceptive, or manipulative acts or practices" in connection with credit-default swaps. Next, the Office of Thrift Supervision would be abolished with the functions performed by that office transferred to the Comptroller of the Currency.

CANADA'S FINANCIAL SYSTEM

In a recent assessment of Canada's financial system, the IMF concluded that Canada's system is highly mature, sophisticated, and well-managed. In addition, the system is characterized by strong prudential regulation and supervision and a well-designed system of deposit insurance and arrangements for crisis management and resolution of failed banks. Supervisory responsibility for the financial sector in Canada is divided among the federal government, among the provincial governments, and among a group of agencies within the federal government. The federal government is responsible for supervising all banks, federally incorporated insurance companies, trust and loan companies, cooperative credit associations and federal pension plans. Regulations separating banks, insurers, trust companies, and investment dealers in Canada were largely eliminated in the 1 980s. Also, by the 1990s, all of the major investment dealers in Canada were owned by banks, which not only created an integrated bank model, it also placed such dealers under close regulatory supervision. Provincial governments are responsible for supervising securities dealers, mutual fund and investment advisors, credit unions, and provincially incorporated trust, loan, and insurance companies. As a result, there are 13 provincial regulatory authorities, each administering securities laws and regulations. The Minister of Finance, however, oversees the incorporation of banks, permitting foreign bank branches, and reviews of large bank mergers. In particular, the Minister has broad discretionary authority to disapprove mergers, which has effectively eliminated such transactions.

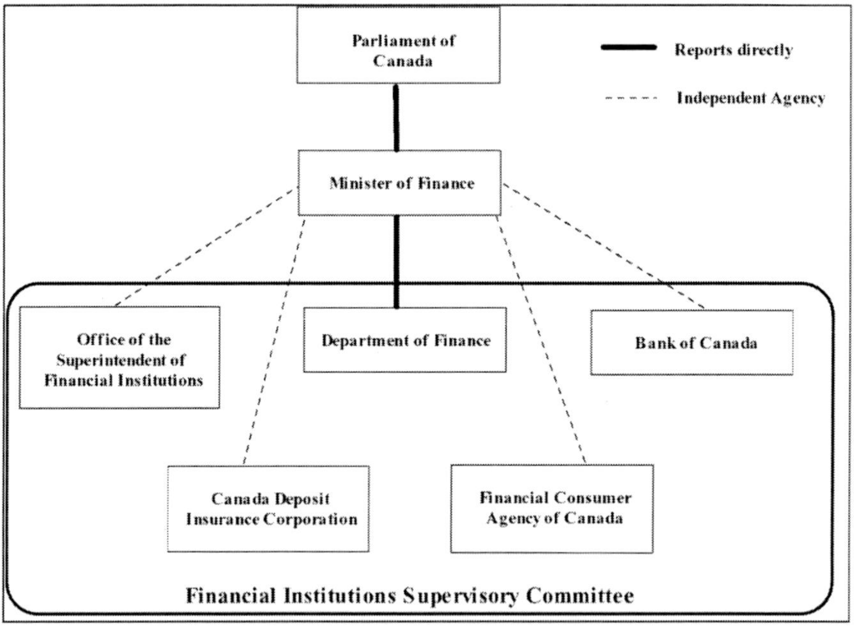

Source: Office of the Superintendent of Financial Institutions.

Figure 2. Canada's Financial System Supervisory Structure

Within the federal government, the Financial Institutions Supervisory Committee (FISC) acts as the chief coordinating body that sets regulatory policy and supervises financial institutions. The Committee is comprised of the Department of Finance of the Ministry of Finance and four independent government agencies: the Office of the Superintendent of Financial Institutions (OSFI); the Bank of Canada; the Canada Deposit Insurance Corporation (CDIC); and the Financial Consumer Agency of Canada (FCAC), as indicated in Figure 2. These five semiofficial agencies report to the Minister of Finance, who is responsible to the Canadian Parliament.

FISC generally meets quarterly, but can meet more often if needed. In addition, FISC conducts a legally mandated five-year review of the National Bank Act to ensure that federal regulatory legislation is modernized periodically. Within FISC, the OSFI plays a key role in supervising Canada's financial sector. The OSFI supervises all domestic banks, branches of foreign banks operating in Canada, trust and loan companies, cooperative credit companies, life insurance companies, and property and casualty insurance companies. The OSFI has set limits on the ability of Canadian banks to leverage their capital and has set target capital ratios that are higher then the international standard. In broad terms, the OSFI is responsible for a number of activities including: 1) assessing the financial conditions and operating performance of the institutions under its jurisdiction; 2) reviewing information obtained from statutory filings, financial reporting, and management reporting requirements; 3) conducting meetings with institutions; 4) attending board meetings when necessary of institutions to discuss the results of supervisory reviews; 5) providing composite risk ratings to institutions; 6) advising institutions of any corrective measures that the institution will be requested to take; 7) monitoring any corrective measures; and 8) reporting to the Minister of Finance on an annual basis.[22]

The OSFI also has considerable enforcement powers, including the authority to intervene progressively in problem institutions under "structured early intervention" provisions that articulate a four-stage process culminating in closure, even while an institution's capital may remain positive. The four-stage process is comprised of the following:

- Stage 1. – **Early Warning.** If an institution has been identified as Stage 1, the OSFI has identified deficiencies in the institutions financial condition, policies, or procedures that could lead the institution to fall into a Stage 2 category where there is the risk of insolvency or failure.
- Stage 2.- **Risk to Financial Viability or Solvency.** At this stage, an institution is judged to pose material safety and soundness concerns and is vulnerable to adverse business and economic conditions.
- Stage 3. – **Future Financial Viability is in Serious Doubt.** At this stage, the OSFI has identified that the institution has failed to remedy the problems that were identified in Stage 2 and the situation is worsening. The situation poses severe safety and soundness concerns and is experiencing problems that pose a material threat to its future

viability or solvency unless effectiveness corrective measures are initiated.

- Stage 4. – **Non-Viability/Insolvency is Imminent.** At this stage, OSFI has determined that the institution is experiencing severe financial difficulties and has deteriorated to such an extent that: 1) the institution has failed to meet regulatory capital requirements; 2) the statutory conditions for taking control have been met; and 3) the institution has failed to develop and implement an acceptable business plan.

In addition, the OSFI plays a key role in regulating Canada's financial sector, providing a nearly unified regulatory and supervisory framework. As is the case with supervision, OSFI is responsible for regulating federal financial institutions, including banks, insurance companies, foreign bank representative offices, and pension plans that are under federal jurisdiction. One weakness of this system is that there are gaps in the regulatory framework concerning such collective investment schemes as mutual funds, where the operators of such funds have not been subject to a registration regime.

The Bank of Canada is responsible primarily for conducting monetary policy by setting interest rate targets and adjusting the supply of credit. The Bank also serves as the key component in the payments system by providing a check clearing function, and it serves as the traditional lender of last resort. In its conduct of monetary policy, the Bank of Canada adopted in 2000 a system of eight pre-set dates per year on which it announces its key policy rate – the target overnight rate of interest. It has veered from these pre-set dates only under exceptional circumstances.[23] While the Bank of Canada reports to the Minister of Finance, this public announcement system acts as an important element in making the Bank's activities transparent to the public and to the financial markets and relatively free from non-economic considerations. The Bank also has three credit facilities at its disposal in its traditional role as the lender of last resort, including a facility to provide liquidity to any financial or nonfinancial firm through outright purchases of a wide range of claims in the event of "severe and unusual stress on a financial market or financial system."

Canada's financial system is dominated by five large banking groups (Royal Bank of Canada, TD Canada Trust, Bank of Nova Scotia, Bank of Montreal, and Canadian Imperial Bank) that account for about 60% of the total assets of Canada's financial sector, as indicated in **Table 6**. In comparison, foreign banks account for about 4% of Canada's total assets in the financial sector.

The low representation by foreign banks is attributed to the "widely-held" rule for large banks that limits the concentration of bank share ownership and, therefore, reduces the scope for mergers and for foreign entry through acquisitions or mergers. This lack of competition, combined with Canada's financial legal framework, allows Canadian banks to concentrate more on their low-risk, profitable domestic retail banking activities (services provided to individuals including: deposits, savings accounts, mortgages, credit cards, etc.), generally leaving large domestic borrowers to conduct their wholesale banking activities (services provided to corporations, governments, and other entities) abroad. Some observers argue that this framework also reduces incentives for innovation among Canada's protected banks and has proved to be difficult for small businesses and venture capitalists. Canada's insurance sector is dominated by three large domestic groups, which account for over 80% of the assets in this sector. The securities sector is marked by large Canadian, as well as U.S. and UK securities firms.

Table 6. Canada: Financial Sector Structure, End-2006

	Assets		
	Billions of $Can.	**Percent of Total Assets**	**Percent of GDP**
Banks	$2,389.0	59.3%	166.0%
Canadian	2,214.0	54.9	153.8
Foreign	175.0	4.3	12.2
Trusts (including bank subsidiaries)	254.7	6.3	17.7
Credit unions	193.8	4.8	13.5
Life insurance companies	346.5	8.6	24.1
Canadian	331.1	8.2	23.0
Foreign	15.4	0.4	1.1
Property and casualty insurance	93.2	2.3	6.5
Mutual funds	660.2	16.4	45.9
Asset based financing and leasing	92.3	2.3	6.4
Total	4,029.7	100.0	280.0

Source: **Canada: Financial System Stability Assessment – Update,** International Monetary Fund, January 15, 2008, p. 11.

Unlike the United States and some European countries, subprime mortgages account for fewer than 5% of Canadian mortgages, which sharply limited Canada's direct exposure to the meltdown that occurred in the subprime mortgage market. Although Canada's mortgage markets are somewhat less innovative than in the United States, Canadian consumers seem to be well served and home ownership rates are comparable with those in the United States.[24] In addition, Canadian law requires that all bank-held mortgages above a loan-to-value ratio of 80% be insured, which has curtailed the securitization of mortgages by banks in Canada. About one-third of mortgages are securitized in Canada, about half as much in percentage terms as in the United States.[25] In addition, prepayment penalties and the lack of interest deductibility reduces the demand for longterm mortgages, so the maturity of most mortgages generally does not exceed 5 to 10 years.

Economic Effects of Canada's Supervisory System

Canada's financial system has been relatively more resilient during the financial crisis compared with counterparts in the United States and Europe. Nevertheless, Canada's financial system has not been immune to the financial crisis nor has it escaped the economic downturn that has stalled global economic growth. The Canadian economy is linked with the international economy. As a result, a sharp drop in exports and a decline in commodity prices have negatively affected the Canadian economy. Household wealth has declined, unemployment is rising, and the economy is expected to post a negative rate of economic growth in 2009, worsening the condition of Canada's financial sector. So far, Canadian banks have suffered a loss of 50% in the value of their equities. Consequently, the banks faced pressure from financial markets to increase their capital ratios, which they apparently did by tapping private sources.

As a result of the financial crisis, aspects of Canada's financial system are being closely scrutinized as the United States considers ways to amend its own financial system to limit the possibility of another financial crisis. However, the smaller scope of Canada's financial system and its economy likely lessen the transferability of systems or procedures used in Canada to the vastly more complex U.S. financial system. In addition, it can be argued that Canada's supervisors and regulators can take a more conservative approach than their

U.S. counterparts as a result of Canada's proximity to the U.S. capital markets. Nevertheless, Canada's financial supervisory system and regulatory structure have proven to be less susceptible to the bank failures that have loomed in the United States and Europe and may offer some insight for U.S. policymakers. Canada's reliance at the federal level on a unified supervisor and regulator appears to have some merits as compared to a more decentralized approach.

Canada's approach does have some drawbacks. Specifically, Canada's system of regulating securities markets at the provincial level means that regulations regarding market participants and investor protection differ by province, creating inefficiencies in the system and raising costs to providers and consumers. Differences between provinces also mean that coordinating policy approaches across the 13 provinces can be slow and cumbersome.

Furthermore, the nature, structure, and powers of the provincial regulators vary, which increases the costs to financial services providers and to consumers, because financial services providers are required to pay fees to the regulatory authorities in all of the provinces where they raise capital. This ultimately raises the cost of capital and limits access to funding. It also inhibits the growth and development of the markets and innovation in developing financial instruments. In addition, while the conservative, risk-adverse approach employed by Canada's banks helped to shield them from some of the current financial turmoil, the approach also reduces efficiency in the market and reduces competition. Acquisitions of Canadian banks are significantly impeded by the rule that bank stocks be widely held and mergers are effectively prohibited. With reduced competitiveness pressures, Canadian banks maintain low-risk balance sheets at the expense of greater innovation and more efficient capital allocation. This approach also means that financing for small firms and venture capital for potentially high-growth companies is sharply reduced.

End Notes

[1] Appelbaum, Binyamin, and Zachary A. Goldfarb, U.S. Weighs Single Agency to Regulate Banking Industry, *The Washington Post*, May 28, 2009, p. A1.

[2] Cho, David, Binyamin Appelbaum, and Zachary A. Goldfarb, Goals Shift For Reform of Financial Regulation, *The Washington Post*, June 10, 2009, p. A1, Cho, David, and Zachary A. Goldfarb, Core Reforms Held Firm As Much Else Fell Away, *The Washington Post*, June 18, 2009, p. A1..

[3] *Monetary Policy Report*, The Bank of Canada, April 2009, p. 19.

[4] *World Economic Outlook*, The International Monetary Fund, April, 2009, p. 69.

[5] Klyuev, Vladimir, *Real Implications of Financial Linkages between Canada and the United States*, IMF Working Paper WP/08/23, International Monetary Fund, January 2008.
[6] *Monetary Policy Report*, the Bank of Canada, April 2009, p. 9-10.
[7] Ibid, p. 22.
[8] *Financial System Review*, the Bank of Canada, June 2009, p. 13.
[9] *Concluding Statement of the IMF's 2009 Article IV Mission to Canada*, International Monetary Fund, press releaser no. 09/73, March 11, 2009.
[10] *Financial System Review*, p. 3.
[11] State-owned corporations at either the federal, state, or territorial level.
[12] *Canada's Economic Action Plan, 2009 Budget*, Chapter 3, Ministry of Finance.
[13] Tier 1 capital is the core measure of a bank's financial strength from a regulator's perspective. It generally is comprised of common stock and disclosed reserves.
[14] Rostnovski, Lev, and Rocco Huang, Why Are Canadian Banks More Resilient? IMF Working Paper WP/09/152. International Monetary Fund, July 2009, , p. 16.
[15] *Financial System Review*, p. 4.
[16] *Concluding Statement on the IMF's 2009 Article IV Mission to Canada*.
[17] *Financial System Review*, p. 1.
[18] Ratnovski, Huang, *Why Are Canadian Banks More Resilient?,* p. 4.
[19] Ibid., p. 11.
[20] For greater detail, see: CRS Report R40249, *Who Regulates Whom? An Overview of U.S. Financial Supervision*, by Mark Jickling and Edward V. Murphy.
[21] Applebaum, Binyamin, By Switching their Charters, Banks Skirt Supervision, *The Washington Post*, January 22, 2009, p. A1.
[22] *Guide to Intervention for Federally Regulated Deposit-Taking Institutions*, Government of Canada.
[23] Macklem, Tiff, Information and Analysis for Monetary Policy: Coming to a Decision, *Bank of Canada Review*, Summer 2002, p. 12.
[24] Kiff, John, *Canadian Residential Mortgage Markets: Boring But Effective?,* IMF Working Paper WP/09/130, International Monetary Fund, June 2009, p. 12.
[25] Ibid, p.5.

In: International Perspectives on Financial… ISBN: 978-1-61728-006-1
Editor: James P. Corrigan © 2011 Nova Science Publishers, Inc.

Chapter 4

FINANCIAL REGULATION AND OVERSIGHT: LATIN AMERICAN FINANCIAL CRISES AND REFORM LESSONS FROM CHILE*

J. F. Hornbeck

SUMMARY

The 111th Congress has taken a broad approach to capturing the lessons on financial crises as part of the effort to evaluate possibilities for revamping the U.S. financial regulatory system. Latin America stands out as one region that has survived multiple financial crises, and in the aftermath of such devastation, many countries undertook comprehensive regulatory reform. Although a smaller developing economy, Chile provides one important example. Following two financial crises, one the result of extreme over regulation, the other of catastrophic under regulation, Chile redesigned its regulatory system in 1986. Since then, it has had one of the most stable financial systems in Latin America and has overcome regional and global financial crises when other countries in the hemisphere did not. In so doing, new-found soundness of the banking system has not compromised bank profitability, reflecting

---

* This is an edited, reformatted and augmented version of a CRS Report for Congress publication dated August 2009.

modernization and efficiency gains that paralleled development of effective prudential regulation and oversight.

Chile's success rests on a 1986 overhaul of the General Banking Act. Conceptually, reform had two fundamental principles: simplify and streamline prudential regulation and supervision. Under the framework developed in the G-30 report, *The Structure of Financial Supervision*, Chile adopted what might be classified as an integrated approach to regulation. The architecture was reshaped, consolidated, and vastly strengthened by giving most regulatory responsibility to the Superintendency of Banks and Financial Institutions (SBIF), with supportive oversight by three other specialized agencies. The SBIF has sweeping oversight powers over "banking enterprises irrespective of their nature and the financial entities whose control is not otherwise entrusted by law to a different institution... [and] shall also be in charge of the supervision of companies whose corporate purpose consists in the issuance or operation of credit cards."

Experience from Chile points to the value of establishing: (1) a strong, independent, and consolidated regulatory and oversight agency, with broad and definitive powers; (2) enhanced transparency through a number of specific reporting measures; (3) clear capital standards that include the 8% minimum Basel risk-weighted capital-asset ratio, capital requirements relative to reserves, deposits, and other liabilities, and total capital equal to at least 3% of total assets; (4) deposit insurance to cover up to 90% of an individual's total deposits capped at a specified limit; and (5) oversight based on a formal bank rating system following the CAMEL standards (capital, asset quality, management, earnings, liquidity, and later bank management), Basel II guidelines, and additional limitations on bank investment activities.

Chile's experience correlates with testimony by three noted economists before the Joint Economic Committee on April 21, 2009, who challenged policy makers to think very differently about how the financial sector should work and be regulated. In addressing the theme of the hearings, each conveyed the pitfalls of the "too big to fail" phenomenon, noting how loose or inappropriate regulation has led to "gargantuan," opaque firms that can be exploitive and highly difficult to regulate. The witnesses argued that only when risk is internalized and the promise of a bailout withheld will behavior begin to change. Chile has protected itself from severe repercussions of the current crisis, in part because of regulations in place that restrict risky behavior and promote a more traditional commercial banking model, although they are no guarantee of perpetual success in avoiding future crises. Still, the link between a sound financial sector and economic growth and development is now well documented, and evidence from Chile some argue suggests that although there may be tradeoffs between efficiency, growth and prudential regulation, over the long run, avoiding a major financial crisis may more than offset the opportunity costs of a more comprehensive regulatory environment, particularly if a proper balance can be achieved.

Effective financial regulation seeks to strike a balance between supporting an efficient and competitive financial market, and ensuring the safety and soundness of the financial system. Too much regulation and the cost of compliance can constrain lending, profitability, innovation, and economic growth. Too little regulation and financial liberalization may result in excessive risk taking. In either case, the outcome may be suboptimal financial intermediation, or perhaps even systemic crisis. Core policy issues are many and interconnected. They include: determining the institutional architecture and level of authority of financial regulation and supervision; setting standards for capital adequacy and deposit insurance; and ensuring operational transparency, with the goal of achieving effective prudential oversight and promotion of timely, coordinated, and successful responses to systemic problems.[1]

The 111th Congress has taken a broad approach to capturing the lessons on financial crises as part of the effort to evaluate possibilities for revamping the U.S. regulatory system. Latin America stands out as one region that has survived multiple financial crises, many of which crippled entire financial sectors. In the aftermath of such devastation, many countries undertook regulatory reform. In the case of Chile, it led to the development of a long-term safe and sound financial system. Although important differences exist between emerging market and developed country economies, insights from Latin American economies can be instructive, and Congress has already taken the lead in fleshing some of them out.[2] This report discusses Latin American financial crises and the lessons from comprehensive regulatory reform undertaken by Chile.

U.S. FINANCIAL DEREGULATION AND THE CURRENT CRISIS

Beginning in 1980, the United States entered a lengthy period of incremental deregulation of the financial sector, for many reasons. In part, this trend reflected an ideological shift toward greater confidence in market-based solutions. Changed macroeconomic conditions, particularly the onset of high inflation in the 1970s, also prompted regulatory reform. Banks and savings and loans (S&Ls or thrifts) had become uncompetitive because of outdated regulations such as interest rate caps on loans and deposits. These types of restrictions caused financial resources to seek higher returns in mutual funds and other less restrictive investment vehicles, threatening the banking and thrift industries.

Congress played an important role in holding hearings and ultimately in passing legislation in the early 1980s that guided deregulation. Within a short time, however, these regulatory changes became controversial. The S&L crisis of the mid-1980s, along with record bank failures, was very much tied to the excessive risk taking of management and myriad other causes. However, they also raised questions about the regulatory system that permitted such excessive risk taking and failed to intervene effectively. In the words of the Federal Deposit Insurance Corporation (FDIC), regulatory changes "were generally unaccompanied by actions to restrict the increased risk taking they made possible and so contributed to bank and thrift failures."[3]

Nonetheless, deregulation continued into the 1990s and beyond. Banks and thrifts took on increasing risk, reducing capital requirements where possible and continuing to lobby for even greater deregulation.[4] Financial liberalization predictably spawned financial markets that became ever more complex, concentrated, and international in scope. Lines began to blur between the types of financial institutions that compete with one another (e.g. banking, insurance, and securities) and the increasingly complex products they came to offer (e.g. collateralized debt obligations, credit default swaps, and other credit derivatives). In addition, the growth of unregulated institutions, such as hedge funds and private equity firms, raised new questions about financial institution risk management and public sector regulation and oversight.[5] This lesson was widely drawn following the collapse of Long-Term Capital Management in 2000.

Despite macroeconomic changes that compelled the need to reconsider prudential regulation, financial liberalization came with clear warnings of the potential for excessive risk taking, both in terms of institutions seeking out the least demanding regulators (regulatory arbitrage), and possible introduction of systemic contagion through consolidation.[6] A quarter century later, in the wake of repeated financial disasters, the United States faces a more severe financial crisis, leaving many to speculate whether past lessons have been adequately incorporated into policy reform aimed at sound regulation of the financial sector. Sparked by the collapse of U.S. housing and credit markets in

2007, the current crisis is widely understood to have been caused by a confluence of trends in deregulation, global integration, and greater use of highly complex and poorly regulated (or understood) financial products. As stated by one leading expert and member of the Federal Reserve Board, the crisis resulted from "massive failures of risk management by financial institutions and of supervision by government authorities."[7] The United States now faces a fundamental question: what should the approach to prudential regulation and supervision of the U.S. financial system look like in the future?

Some may be tempted to suggest at this point that greater restriction on financial institutions at both the national and international levels is needed. Evidence from many studies suggests, however, that the answer is likely to be more nuanced for three reasons. First, notwithstanding the positive effects of steps taken to address regulatory inconsistencies internationally through the Basel accords,[8] most financial crises arise from domestic market distortions, weak institutions, and inadequate national policies. Second, countries with weak overall government and ureaucratic systems tend to default to policies that overly restrict financial institutions. Third, although seemingly counterintuitive, some cross-country research suggests that countries with the most highly restrictive regulations encourage less diversified operations, which in turn can increase firm inefficiency and the risk of a financial crisis.[9] Therefore, with respect to regulation, more is not necessarily better.

FINANCIAL REGULATORY MODELS[10]

The Group of Thirty (G-30) released a comprehensive review of financial regulatory models in 2008. It presents a useful typology of financial regulatory models (approaches) based on 17 major countries representing both developing and more advanced economies. The study condenses them into four basic models:

- the Institutional approach: the firm's legal status (bank, broker-dealer, or insurance company) determines which regulator oversees both safety and soundness as well as business conduct of the enterprise, often leading to multiple regulators;
- the Functional approach: the firm's type of business determines the regulator, irrespective of its legal status, each type of business might have a separate regulator;

- the Integrated approach: the firm is subject to "a single universal regulator," that conducts all oversight work; and
- the Twin Peaks approach: the firm is supervised by two agencies, one responsible for safety and soundness, another for conduct-of-business regulation.

The G-30 report notes that there are some key issues that transcend the four regulatory models and that each approach to regulation has its benefits and costs. First, regulatory structures usually arise from the particular economic and political circumstances of the country, often in the wake of a crisis that has exposed the failures of the model in use. Second, no model is unabashedly recommended for all countries. Third, both the Institutional and Functional approaches present problems of communication, coordination, and jurisdictional conflict, and may be falling out of practice in many countries, particularly in light of the trend toward industry concentration. Some countries, however, are still successfully employing one of these two models. Fourth, the Integrated and Twin Peaks models may be coming into vogue, given inherent weaknesses in multi-regulator models. Unifying oversight is one of the primary reasons these two models are receiving more attention, but the single regulator model comes with its own cautions with respect to ensuring that adequate checks and balances are in place and guaranteeing freedom from problems of coordination and intra-agency jurisdictional squabbles.

Latin American Financial Crises and the United States

As small open economies, Latin American countries are much different from the United States and other developed countries, making it important to note some key distinctions related to financial crises. Latin American crises have typically involved deep fiscal deficits, poor prospects for servicing debt, questionable macroeconomic and exchange rate policies, and weak institutions. Collectively these factors have contributed to the self-fulfilling nature of the classic Latin American financial crisis, in which investors (often led by home country elites) typically flee a particular country at the early onset of a problem, causing exchange rate collapses, exacerbated debt problems, and destabilized financial markets (stock and bond markets, banks, and credit markets). Latin American countries can also be vulnerable to external shocks and contagion, an example being the 1998 financial crisis in Brazil, often associated with contagion following foreign capital retreats from Russia and Asia during the previous year.

The United States is not subject to this same type of panic and is better equipped to adopt countervailing policies, so the lessons related to addressing contagion, exchange rate policies, and fiscal excess are not directly relevant. Nonetheless, a key lesson that has emerged from extensive research into Latin American financial crises of the 1 980s and 1990s is that domestic market distortions and policy failures in the financial sector were a part of many crises, more so than external shocks and negative repercussions from international financial integration.[11] Also, financial crises, irrespective of their proximate causes or country of origin, tend to unfold in predictably similar ways, devastating asset markets, output and employment levels, and public indebtedness.[12]

As a starting point, the 1980s debt crisis in Latin America represents an unusual episode for both the United States and Latin America. Unlike crises that would follow, this one involved heavy sovereign indebtedness to U.S. banks, reflecting what would become a disturbing nexus between emerging market financial crises and financial liberalization in the United States. U.S. bank exposure to Latin American debt was one example of the increased risk taking in the 1 980s by a quickly expanding and consolidating U.S. financial sector in search of new profit opportunities in an increasingly deregulated environment. In fact, the size of the bank debt was so large relative to capital as to imperil some major money center banks. This group included Citicorp, which not only led the charge in acquiring risky Latin American assets, but did the same for "toxic assets" prior to the current crisis.[13] In response, the U.S. Government, including Congress, intervened, not only to help contain crises in major defaulters like Mexico and Brazil, but also to ensure that important U.S. financial institutions did not fail.[14]

Analysts later pointed to flagrant risk taking (or questionable risk management skills) on the parts of institutions in Latin America and the United States that operated largely unchecked. In the case of the United States, this analysis raised doubts about U.S. regulatory efforts even by the regulators themselves, which would eventually encourage Congress to pass legislation requiring uniform, risk-weighted capital requirements for all banks in the United States. This episode also helped prioritize the development of international capital adequacy standards (Basel I), again with the strong encouragement from Congress.[15]

As history has demonstrated, however, U.S. financial institutions would later find new ways to increase profitability in a more relaxed regulatory environment. In Latin America, however, such creative market responses were not pursued, or done so with more oversight. Following their own banking crises in the 1980s, many countries in the region concentrated on financial sector reform with a central focus on reducing risk, preferring to err on the side of prudential supervision. Although vilified by some for accepting the higher opportunity costs, others have argued that the trade off is in part responsible for some notable successes in achieving long-term stability by re-engineering regulatory systems, including surviving the current economic downturn far better than many observers would have thought possible. [16]

Financial Sector Reform in Latin America

Although Latin American countries have longstanding equity and bond markets, and some have well-developed futures markets and nascent derivatives exchanges, by and large, they are far less sophisticated than their U.S. counterparts. Privatization and exchange of equity in corporations on a widespread basis is a fairly recent phenomenon, not developing significantly until after the debt crisis of the 1 980s. Even today, while far more robust than in the past, trading remains relatively concentrated and influenced by the state either directly through ownership, or indirectly through regulatory or legal (even constitutional) constraints.[17] Bond markets in Latin America have played an important role in attracting foreign financing in the post-1982 crisis period, but international investors generally have insisted on bonds denominated in major international currencies, and in domestic markets, bonds are used less frequently with the exception of large corporate borrowers.[18]

Because banking is by far the largest element of the financial sector, its regulation has the fullest history to draw on. Prudential regulation and bank supervision experiences have varied considerably among Latin American countries, but one overarching trend has been convergence to international or developed country standards, largely in response to past financial crises.[19] As important as improvements in regulatory and supervisory structures have been, they are also considered incomplete and the current global recession is an important test of these new standards.

By historical standards, the ability of many Latin American countries to avoid major financial instability during the current crisis has been striking.

Macroeconomic policies have played an important role. The movement toward flexible exchange rates, in particular, is a major change from previous periods of crisis. This has allowed currency depreciations to do much of the adjustment work, freeing up monetary policy to fulfill, to varying degrees, a traditional countercyclical role (reducing interest rates) often not possible in previous crises. In addition, most Latin American countries have taken steps to support banking systems by maintaining high levels of international reserves, directly increasing liquidity to the private sector, easing reserve requirements, and providing alternative financing to the corporate sector.[20]

Undoubtedly, financial systems in Latin America are, on average, more robust than in the past. As reported by the International Monetary Fund (IMF), the starting conditions of Latin American banks, on average, were healthy as the current crisis unfolded. Capital-asset ratios were sound (15%, nearly double the 8% standard defined in the Basel II accord), returns on equity high (20%), and liquidity ratios "adequate" for "non-crisis situations." Bank balance sheets were healthy. They had adequate levels of domestic deposits, few toxic assets, and only light exposure to derivatives, mostly in the large banks.[21]

In part, the health of Latin American financial systems reflects what the IMF calls successful "first generation" reform of financial regulation. In evaluating Latin America's compliance with Basel core principles, however, the IMF notes that these countries may wish to take the next step given they are only 60% compliant with eight core principles that are virtually fully adopted by developed countries. In addition, many Latin American countries still have many systemically important institutions that may not be adequately regulated, including many nonbank financial institutions.[22] In attempting to gauge any lessons from Latin America, therefore, it is perhaps best to consider the most pertinent examples of financial sector regulatory reform, of which Chile is a prime candidate, despite noted differences with the United States.

Chile: Financial Crisis and the Long Road to Prudential Regulatory Reform

By all accounts, Chile has had one of the most stable financial systems in Latin America for the past quarter century, the product of major changes to its banking law in 1986. In the aftermath of two financial crises, the first that resulted from macroeconomic policy failures that were exacerbated under a system of over regulation, the second directly related to catastrophic under regulation, Chile redesigned its financial regulatory system. Since then, Chile's financial sector has overcome many regional and global financial crises when other countries in the hemisphere could not. In so doing, soundness of the banking system has not compromised bank profitability, reflecting modernization, efficiency gains, and increased competition that paralleled development of effective prudential regulation and oversight.[23] Because regulation and oversight of the U.S. system is being heavily scrutinized, some lessons from Chile may be instructive as Congress grapples with various policy alternatives.

Early Failures in Chilean Financial Regulatory Reform

From 1930 until 1973, Chile lived under a highly regulated financial system including interest rate controls and quantitative restrictions on credit. From 1970 to 1973, under Chile's short-lived "socialist experiment," the state had virtually full control of banks. This system imploded as part of a broader economic collapse in 1973, which was due largely to poor policy choices that led to severe macroeconomic imbalances. The financial sector suffered deeply and because of heavy state control, was poorly positioned to respond to economic shocks. Regulation was also cumbersome and fragmented. Chile had adopted a Functional approach to regulation, having agencies assigned to oversee financial institutions based largely on their type of business – commercial lending, insurance, mortgages, and securities.

Following the 1973 crisis, Chile undertook a wholesale change in economic management, including financial reform that transformed a model based on state control to one relying on market discipline combined with light regulation.[24] Supervision was consolidated in the Superintendency of Banks and Financial Institutions (Superintendencia de Bancos E Instituciones Financieras – SBIF), but an ideological bias against strong regulation and lack of resources "discouraged the SBIF from taking an active regulatory stance."[25] Banks were privatized, regulations loosened (e.g., reserve requirements lowered, interest rate ceilings removed, limitations on foreign banking softened), and prudential supervision relaxed, resulting in ineffective oversight. The scope of financial institutions became more expansive; commercial, investment, mortgage, pension fund, and development institutions operated in many of the same markets, offering a variety of the same products.

As happened in many developed and developing countries in the 1980s following banking liberalization, deregulation led to a rapid increase in bank credit and capital market deepening. In Chile, it was further enhanced by relaxed rules on foreign banking and forced saving through pension reform. A number of inherent problems, however, eventually surfaced. Expansive credit led to asset bubbles, not unlike what the United States experienced in 2007.[26] Of particular concern to regulators, privatization encouraged industry consolidation dominated by conglomerates, which would prove difficult to supervise. The government also agreed to sell state-owned banks to conglomerates, financing as much as 90% with public funds. This policy compounded the problem by creating opaque conglomerates (*grupos*) with highly leveraged financial subsidiaries. In addition, banking law allowed for intra-conglomerate lending so that by June 1982, as Chile tipped into financial crisis, some 21% of loans held by the five largest banks were made to firms within the same *grupo*.[27] In many cases, this amounted to rolling over unrealized loan losses, which eventually contributed to bank insolvency. [28]

These policies and practices not only produced highly leveraged financial institutions, but they failed to curtail illegal practices in bank lending that increased risk taking, circumvented prudential oversight, and eventually led to the collapse of the financial sector. For example, to avoid restrictions on intra-conglomerate lending, the *grupos* created shell corporations, operating both within Chile and abroad to funnel loans to intra-group subsidiaries. These corporations also sold stocks among themselves in sufficiently large quantities so as to raise share prices above the market value. These stocks were then used as collateral for loans to buy banks.[29]

Analyses point to the government's role in compounding these "conduct of business" problems by agreeing to the rescue of a major bank in 1976, an act that was widely interpreted as an implicit open-ended guarantee of all deposits in the banking system. This further encouraged imprudent behavior by banks and diluted market discipline.[30] Depositors had little incentive to scrutinize their bank. In short, the regulatory regime was circumvented and ultimately failed. It has been characterized by one specialist as "one of the world's weakest regulatory systems, operating with unwarranted confidence in the strength of the banking sector coupled with a lack of adequate supervision."[31]

The faltering economy exposed the over leveraged financial system and weak regulatory structure. Although the Chilean Congress passed the first banking law requiring diversification away from *grupo* self-financing in August 1981, it was too late. [32] Non-performing loans rose to a huge 113% of capital and reserves and in the end, beginning in November 1981, the government intervened with a massive rescue package involving 60% of the combined sector's loan portfolio. The bank bailout was managed by the Central Bank of Chile and focused on a three-tier strategy: (1) debt restructuring for commercial and household borrowers; (2) purchases of non-performing loans from financial institutions; and (3) the expeditious sale, merger, or liquidation of distressed institutions. Chile's aggressive actions succeeded in correcting a systemic crisis in the financial system and restoring the banking system to complete health within four years.[33] The important lessons for regulatory reform, however, came in the years that followed.[34]

Financial Sector Reform in Chile: the General Banking Act and Strengthening of Prudential Supervision and Regulation

During the 1980s, Chile modified its banking laws, regulatory structure, and oversight practices in ways that would lead to a widely regarded improvement in the stability of the country's financial sector.[35] The basis for Chile's success by many accounts rests with a 1986 overhaul of the General Banking Act (GBA). The GBA remains the governing statute, last revised in June 2007. It sought a middle path by providing a strong and well-defined prudential regulation within a market-based economy. The overall goal was to strike a balance between two extreme regulatory models that had failed, each in their own way, to provide a transparent and credible oversight structure. Reforms also eliminated or restricted many of the practices that were directly responsible for the 1981-83 financial crisis, particularly lending among affiliated companies.

Conceptually, Chile's comprehensive reform had two fundamental principles: simplify and streamline prudential regulation and supervision. Under the G-30 report framework for financial regulation, Chile adopted what might be classified as an integrated approach to regulation. The architecture was reshaped, consolidated, and vastly strengthened by giving most regulatory responsibility to one agency, the Superintendency of Banks and Financial Institutions (SBIF). This priority arose from concerns over the previous system that had failed to prevent excesses in the financial system. The new structure also placed supportive regulatory responsibility in three other agencies: the Central Bank of Chile (Banco Central de Chile); the Superintendency of Pensions (Superintendencia de Pensiones – SP); and the Superintendency of Securities and Insurance (Superintendencia de Valores y Seguros – SVS).

Each, however, looks to the SBIF as the primary regulator and supervisory institution of banks and their financial subsidiaries.

By way of example, the Central Bank works cooperatively with the SBIF, supporting the banking system with its discount window and role as lender of last resort. Although it has selective off-site oversight responsibilities (e.g., balance of payments and foreign exchange issues), a 1989 amendment to the banking law restricts the Central Bank's duties largely to monetary policy. The pension system, a major investor in banks, has a separate regulator under the SP, but it relies heavily on the SBIF for information. The SVS is responsible for oversight of brokerages, stock exchanges, securities dealers, mutual funds, and other investment related firms. As is common, however, where securities and insurance firms are organized as subsidiaries of banks or other financial institutions, their oversight falls to the SBIF.[36] The three superintendencies meet to coordinate regulation as part of the Financial Area Superintendents Committee, but the lead agency remains the SBIF.[37]

In addition to consolidating regulation and oversight largely in a newly strengthened SBIF, the 1986 reform gave it vastly new powers to conduct its business. As stated in the General Banking Act, the Superintendent is appointed by the President of the Republic, and the SBIF has sweeping oversight powers for "banking enterprises irrespective of their nature and the financial entities whose control is not otherwise entrusted by law to a different institution... [and] shall also be in charge of the supervision of companies whose corporate purpose consists in the issuance or operation of credit cards." The SBIF has authority: (1) "to examine, without any restriction whatsoever" institutions to ensure compliance with laws, regulations, by-laws and other provisions that apply; (2) to issue instructions to institutions to correct any irregularities; and (3) to impose fines or restrictions on banking activities (e.g., granting or renewal of loans) of institutions not in compliance. Authority is extended to include all subsidiaries of banks that may be in nonbanking financial services and was further extended in 2005 to the derivatives market as well, to promote a comprehensive and coordinated approach to prudential supervision.[38]

POSSIBLE LESSONS FROM THE CHILEAN CASE

Because Chile experienced two financial crises between 1973 and 1981 under two extreme regulatory systems, followed by nearly 25 years of financial stability after implementing major reforms, some argue it showcases the merits of a balanced and comprehensive model of financial regulation and oversight. Of particular note, most of the major principles illuminated by the G-30 report, *The Structure of Financial Supervision*, were identified and formed the basis for reform in Chile over two decades earlier. Specific policy responses and some lessons they drew on are summarized below.

Regulatory Structure

Chile stopped short of instituting a pure Integration approach or single regulator model, but it did react to the failures of ineffective regulation by creating a strong, independent, and consolidated regulatory and oversight agency in the SBIF. As an independent agency, it has broad and definitive powers over a financial system dominated by large bank conglomerates with multiple subsidiaries operating in nonbank finance (securities, insurance, and derivatives). This highly centralized regulatory system has so far appeared to have improved accountability in the financial institutions industry, the success of which may be seen in the sector's ability to weather the current global recession sparked by financial serious shocks in developed economies.[39] Cooperation with the Central Bank and coordination with the other three regulatory agencies via a special inter-agency committee follows the guidelines offered in the 2008 G-30 report. The G-30 report also argues that domestic coordination and communication are critical elements of effective regulation and that the Integrated or Twin Peaks approaches may be better solutions for regulating current business models with diverse financial services and products.

Transparency

Transparency dominated concerns of Chile's regulatory shortfalls. In the 1980s, the activities of large financial conglomerates, many of them illegal even under the then existing system, were largely opaque, contributing to excessive risk taking and ultimately the failure of many large banks. Chilean banking law now requires a number of specific reporting measures to ensure reasonable institution and system transparency. First, the SBIF must publish detailed information on the type and quality of each financial institution it supervises at least three times per year. Second, loan information must be transmitted electronically to the SBIF on a daily basis. Third, loan losses must be recognized on a timely basis, without exception. Fourth, banks are rated annually by two independent private auditors. One key lesson from Chile is that without readily available information, there was little basis for either market or regulatory discipline, leaving financial institutions free to operate solely on their internal decision making process. This can introduce systemic fragility if banks have little confidence in each other when shocks occur.[40]

Capital Adequacy Standards

Capital adequacy standards are still considered the first line of defense for protecting bank safety and soundness.[41] Chile tightened and clarified its standards in the GBA. In addition to the standard 8% minimum Basel risk-weighted capital-asset ratio, Chilean banks have to meet capital requirements relative to reserves, deposits, and other liabilities. Capital must equal at least 3% of total assets.[42] Non-compliance can result in limitations placed on loan and investment activities. These standards were a response to overly leveraged banks during the 1980s crisis. In fact, Chile's banking culture seems to have opted for maintaining capital standards well in excess of the minimum prescribed by Basel II, contributing to confidence in (and stability of) the financial system over the long run.

Deposit Insurance

Given the history of bank bailouts in Chile, it was necessary to change expectations of an implicit government guarantee of all deposits. The 1986 law limited deposit insurance to accounts payable on sight and those of small depositors. Perhaps taking a page from U.S. regulations, it was later expanded to cover up to 90% of an individual's total deposits in the banking system to a specified limit.[43] Chile was able to find a balance that conveyed security to the depositors, thereby guarding against bank runs, and that limited the public commitment, thereby ensuring that depositors still had an incentive to scrutinize banks.

Bank Supervision

Oversight is based on a formal bank rating system following the CAMEL standards (capital, asset quality, management, earnings, liquidity, and later bank management), Basel II guidelines, and additional limitations on bank investment activities (e.g. equity capital, agricultural land). Banks may extend their services through subsidiaries to include securities brokerage, investment fund management, mutual funds, real estate, and financial leasing, all subject to review by the SBIF.[44] Capital requirements already exceed those of the international Basel accord. More sophisticated derivatives are either carefully limited or not permitted. Monitoring falls to the primary financial sector regulatory agency.

CONCLUSIONS: CHILE'S RELEVANCE TO THE UNITED STATES

Testimony before the Joint Economic Committee on April 21, 2009 by three noted economists challenged policy makers to think very differently about how the financial sector should work and be regulated. In addressing the theme of the hearings, each conveyed the pitfalls of the "too big to fail" phenomenon, noting how loose or inappropriate regulation has led to "gargantuan," opaque firms that can be exploitive and difficult to regulate. They all pointed out that, in one form or another, a new approach to regulation should emphasize scaling back the size and scope of certain financial institutions, limiting risk-taking options of these institutions (e.g. types of products and services they can offer), and codifying clear rules of oversight and resolution to make sure all institutions understand that they will bear the cost of bad decisions and behavior. The witnesses argued that only when risk is internalized and the promise of a bailout withheld will behavior begin to change.[45]

The lessons from Chile bear out all these points. The existing prudential regulatory and oversight system has so far limited these types of mistakes from being repeated and is credited with helping maintain the health of the banking sector during the global financial crisis. It continues to update regulations to stay current with a dynamic and innovative industry so as to balance competitiveness with prudence. The result, in 2009 Chile has one of the most stable banking systems among emerging market countries, as evidenced by its capacity to withstand external shocks related to the global recession and international credit contraction. Profitability has declined slightly as loan loss reserves have been increased in response to higher credit risk. But these same measures ensured that the banking industry as a whole has an average capital adequacy ratio above 12%, similar to that of the United States. The portfolio quality of banks is high and yet the banking industry has an annual average return on equity of 15% over the past decade, also equal to or exceeding that of the United States in recent years. Market confidence in the sector may be seen in consistently high bank stock prices and credit ratings on debt securities.[46]

In particular, Chile has protected itself from severe repercussions of the current crisis, which, many argue, is no accident given the regulations in place that improve accountability by restricting risky behavior, enhancing transparency, and promoting a more traditional commercial banking model. For example, the derivatives market deals mostly with interest rate and exchange rate options, which are highly regulated. Banks are not authorized to issue credit derivatives. Chile represents only 3% of securitization activity in Latin America compared to Mexico's 40% and Brazil's 32%. Off-balance sheet exposure is considered only moderate. To the contrary, loans constitute 70% of assets and are originated and administered on the balance sheet. Half of all liabilities are retail or time deposits. The SBIF monitors this system carefully and it is widely understood that noncompliance will be addressed.[47] This situation does not guarantee that a full- proof financial regulatory system is possible, or that Chile will perpetually avoid and future financial crisis. It does, however, point to a very positive exception in a region with a lengthy history of financial crises.

The United States has a far more complex financial sector than Chile. Chile's financial regulatory system could not replace that of the United States. Nonetheless, the broader lessons may be worth consideration because the benefits reach beyond the financial sector. Because it has remained healthy, the financial sector has not pulled Chile into a deep recession, and it appears to be recovering from the global downturn. The link between a sound financial sector and economic growth and development is now well documented, and evidence from Chile, many argue, suggests that although there may be tradeoffs between efficiency, growth and prudential regulation, over the long run, avoiding a major financial crisis may more than offset the opportunity costs of a more comprehensive regulatory environment, particularly if a proper balance can be achieved.

End Notes

[1] More broadly, financial institution regulation may be defined as seeking to achieve safety and soundness of financial institutions, the mitigation of systemic risk, fairness and efficiency of markets, and protection of customers and investors. Group of Thirty, *The Structure of Financial Supervision: Approaches and Challenges in a Global Marketplace*, October 2008, pp. 21-22.

[2] U.S. Congress, Joint Economic Committee, *Too Big to Fail or Too Big to Save? Examining the Systemic Threats of Large Financial Institutions*, 111th Cong., 1st sess., April 21, 2009. See testimony of Professor Simon Johnson.

[3] Federal Deposit Insurance Corporation, *History of the Eighties, Lessons for the Future: An Examination of the Banking Crises of the 1980s and Early 1990s* (Washington, D.C.: FDIC, 1997), p. 10.

[4] Requirements to increase capital reserves, which reduce institutional risk, were met with countervailing tactics. For example, banks increased securitization of debt and altered loan (asset) portfolios in ways that allowed them to actually reduce capital reserves. Reinicke, Wolfgang H., *Banking, Politics and Global Finance: American Commercial Banks and Regulatory Change, 1980-1990* (Washington, D.C.: The Brookings Institution, 1995), pp. 139-140. Also, after much debate and lobbying, Congress eventually revised or eliminated restrictions in some banking laws, such as the Glass-Steagall Act, which had separated commercial and investment banking since the 1930s.

[5] FDIC, op. cit., pp. 10 and 20-21, and Reinicke, op. cit., p. 2.

[6] Reinicke, op. cit., pp. 2-3 and 53. Financial sector integration can create transparency and other problems that make oversight difficult, ultimately leading the "too big to fail" and other issues that can have system-wide repercussions.

[7] Daniel K. Tarullo, *Banking on Basel: The Future of International Financial Regulation* (Washington, D.C.: Peterson Institute for International Economics, 2008), pp. 4 and 8.

[8] The Basel accords are an agreement among participating countries to adopt a framework for setting capital adequacy standards of banks. Basel II was completed in 2004, and a final rule for implementation in the United States was issued on December 7, 2007. See: CRS Report RL34485, *Basel II in the United States: Progress Toward a Workable Framework*, by Walter W. Eubanks.

[9] James R. Barth, Gerard Caprio, Jr., and Ross Levine, "Financial Regulation and Performance: Cross-Country Evidence," in *Banking, Financial Integration, and International Crises*, ed. Leonardo Hernández and Klaus SchmidtHebbel (Santiago: Central Bank of Chile, 2002), pp. 128-136.

[10] Group of Thirty, *The Structure of Financial Supervision,* pp. 24-25. The Group of Thirty comprises leading representatives of the private and public sectors, and academia dedicated to deepening the understanding of international economic and financial issues, particularly with respect to repercussions of policy choices. See: http://www.group30.org/

[11] Leonardo Hernandez and Klaus Schmidt-Hebbel, "Banking, Financial Integration, and International Crises: An Overview," in *Banking, Financial Integration, and International Crises*, ed. Leonardo Hernandez and Klaus SchmidtHebbel, vol. 3 (Santiago: Banco Central de Chile, 2003). In addition, the limited role of international financial integration on credit markets is explored in a paper that finds no relationship between adoption of Basel I capital requirements and later periods of credit crunch in Latin America. Adolfo Barajas, Ralph Chami, and Tomas Cosimano. "Did the Basel Accord Cause a Credit Slowdown in Latin America?" Working Paper WP/05/39, International Monetary Fund. Washington, D.C. February 2005.

[12] Reinhart, Carmen M. and Kenneth S. Rogoff, "The Aftermath of Financial Crises." in *American Economic Review: Papers & Proceedings 2009*, (Pittsburgh: American Economic Association, 2009), pp. 466-472.

[13] FDIC, *History of the Eighties, Lessons for the Future: An Examination of the Banking Crises of the 1980s and Early 1990s*, p. 191-210. This was a time of unprecedented bank failures in the United States, in part because of their efforts to increase profitability by increasing risk as bank regulation was being relaxed. Economic shocks would soon expose the weaknesses of this strategy. Like the current crisis, banks and thrifts also pursued commercial real estate lending "aggressively" while "a pervasive relaxation of underwriting standards took place, unchecked either by the real estate appraisal system or by supervisory constraints." pp. 3-5, 26.

[14] Tarullo, op. cit., pp. 36-37 and Reinicke, op. cit., pp. 134-136 and 142-146. Mexico alone defaulted on $81 billion of debt, some $23 billion held by U.S. banks (p. 142). Through U.S. and IMF efforts first to reschedule debt payments and later provide debt relief, the major money center banks were given time to shore up their balance sheets and eventually wrote off sizable losses. FDIC, op. cit., pp. 43-44.

[15] Reinicke, op. cit., p. 199-200 argues that the combination of a systemic threat to the U.S. banking system and insufficient, if not negligent, regulation actually "mobilized Congress to participate in the debate over capital adequacy and shifted the distribution of political power in the policy network towards the legislature."

[16] Tarullo, pp. 38-39, and Reinicke, pp. 144 and 162-164, especially on the priority of strengthening and harmonizing capital adequacy standards.

[17] Kathryn C. Lavelle, *The Politics of Equity Finance in Emerging Markets* (Oxford: Oxford University Press, 2004), pp. 93-112.

[18] Eduardo Borensztein, Kevin Cowan, Barry Eichengreen, and Ugo Panizza, "Building Bond Markets in Latin America," in *Bond Markets in Latin America*, ed. Eduardo Borensztein, Kevin Cowan, Barry Eichengreen, and Ugo Panizza (Cambridge: The MIT Press, 2008), pp. 1-3.

[19] Jorge Ivan Canales-Kriljenko, *Regional Economic Outlook: Western Hemisphere*, International Monetary Fund, Washington, D.C., May 2009, p. 51-52. Crises have been thc major incentive for reform in the United States as well. See: CRS Report R40249, *Who Regulates Whom? An Overview of U.S. Financial Supervision*, by Mark Jickling and Edward V. Murphy.

[20] International Monetary Fund, op. cit., pp. 17-19.

[21] Ibid., pp. 51-52.

[22] Ibid., pp. 52-61. The eight Basel core principles summarized are: overall compliance; licensing and structure; objectives, independence, transparency, and cooperation; prudential regulation and requirements; methods of ongoing banking supervision; accounting and disclosure; corrective and remedial power of supervisors; and consolidated cross- border banking supervision.

[23] From 2000 to 2004, the Chilean banking system maintained a capital adequacy ratio of 13.5%, notably higher than the 8% minimum recommended by the Basel accords. It also had a return on equity of 15.6%, far more than other countries, including the United States. This combination of positive results was achieved even as interest rate spreads declined, reflecting greater operational efficiency. Cristina Betancour, José de Gregorio, and Alejandro Jara, *Improving the Banking System: the Chilean Experience*, Bank of International Settlements, BIS Papers No 28, Basel, December 2005, p. 169.

[24] Andrés Velasco, "The Chilean Financial System, 1975-85," in *Banking Crises: Cases and Issues*, ed. V. Sundararajan and Tomás J.T. Baliño (Washington, D.C.: International Monetary Fund, 1991), pp. 165, and 120-12 1 and p. 117-120 and Francisco Gallego and Norman Loayza, *Financial Structure in Chile: Macroeconomic Developments and Microeconomic Effects*, Banco Central de Chile, July 2000, pp. 5-7.

[25] Boris Kozolchyk and Heinz P. Rudolph, *Transparency and Truth in Latin American Banking* (Tucson: The National Law Center for Inter-American Free Trade, 2001), p. 81.

[26] These types of assets bubbles have occurred in many countries over time, including the United States on more than one occasion.

[27] Velasco, op. cit., pp. 135-136.

[28] Sergio de la Cuadra and Salvador Valdés, "Myths and Facts about Financial Liberalization in Chile: 1974-1983," in *If Texas Were Chile: A Primer on Banking Reform*, ed. Philip L. Brock (San Francisco: ICS Press, 1992), pp. 38-39, 90.

[29] Velasco, op. cit., p. 135.

[30] Ibid., p. 136 and 151 and Gallego and Loayza, *Financial Structure in Chile: Macroeconomic Developments and Microeconomic Effects*, pp. 5-7.

[31] Kozolchyk and Rudolph, op., cit., p. 80. Law Center for Inter-American Free Trade, 2001), p. 81.

[26] These types of assets bubbles have occurred in many countries over time, including the United States on more than one occasion.

[27] Velasco, op. cit., pp. 135-136.

[28] Sergio de la Cuadra and Salvador Valdés, "Myths and Facts about Financial Liberalization in Chile: 1974-1983," in *If Texas Were Chile: A Primer on Banking Reform*, ed. Philip L. Brock (San Francisco: ICS Press, 1992), pp. 38-39, 90.

[29] Velasco, op. cit., p. 135.

[30] Ibid., p. 136 and 151 and Gallego and Loayza, *Financial Structure in Chile: Macroeconomic Developments and Microeconomic Effects*, pp. 5-7.

[31] Kozolchyk and Rudolph, op., cit., p. 80.

[32] de la Cuadra and Valdés, op. cit., p. 88.

[33] This is in keeping with the "protracted" nature of recessions caused by financial crises, see Reinhart and Rogoff, op. cit., p. 466.

[34] Velasco, op. cit., pp. 113, 140, and 151. Other causes of Chile's crisis include the 1981-82 U.S. recession, and Chile's large macroeconomic imbalances, excessive indebtedness, and incongruous policy responses. For a discussion of the crisis and its resolution, see: CRS Report RS22961, *The U.S. Financial Crisis: Lessons From Chile*, by J. F. Hornbeck.

[35] This effort was part of a comprehensive economic reform program. See: Vittorio Corbo, Leonardo Hernández, and Fernando Parro, *Institutions, Economic Policies and Growth: Lessons from the Chilean Experience*, Banco Central de Chile, Working Paper 317, Santiago, April 2005, pp. 17-19.

[36] GBA, Art. 70, General SVS law, and Kozolchyk and Rudolph, op. cit., p. 86.

[37] Kozolchyk and Rudolph, op. cit., p. 101.

[38] GBA, Art. 1, 12, 20, and 22.

[39] Banco Central de Chile, *Financial Stability Reports, First Half 2009.* Santiago, July 2009.

[40] GBA, Art. 1, 12, 20, and 22. See also: Kozolchyk and Rudolph, op. cit., pp. 80-83 and 97-98, and Velasco, op. cit. pp. 165-167.

[41] Tarullo, op. cit., p. 15.

[42] GBA, Art. 66.

[43] Kozolchyk and Rudolph, op. cit., p. 84. GBA, Art. 144.

[44] Ibid., pp. 86 and 101.

[45] See testimony of Joseph E. Stiglitz, Simon Johnson, and Thomas M. Hoenig. U.S. Congress, Joint Economic Committee, *Too Big to Fail or To Big to Save? Examining the Systemic Threats of Large Financial Institutions*, 111th Cong., 1st sess., April 21, 2009. Available at: *http://jec.senate.gov/*

[46] Banco Central de Chile, *Financial Stability Reports, Second Half 2008 and First Half 2009.* Santiago, January and July 2009, and International Monetary Fund, *Chile: 2008 Article IV Consultation*, Washington, D.C., July 2008, pp. 15- 16 and 28-29.

[47] Banco Central de Chile, *Financial Stability Report, Second Half 2008.* Santiago, January 2009.

CHAPTER SOURCES

The following chapters have been previously published:

Chapter 1 – This is and edited, reformatted and augmented version of a Congressional Research Service publication, Report R40249, dated December 14, 2009.

Chapter 2 – This is and edited, reformatted and augmented version of a Congressional Research Service publication, Report R40788, dated November 20, 2009.

Chapter 3 – This is and edited, reformatted and augmented version of a Congressional Research Service publication, Report R40687, dated November 25, 2009.

Chapter 4 – This is and edited, reformatted and augmented version of a Congressional Research Service publication, Report R40751, dated August 11, 2009.

INDEX

C

F

G

H

M

N

O

P

R

S

T

U

V

W